Mike Holt's

BUSINESS
MANAGEMENT SKILLS

Workbook

Since 1974
www.MikeHolt.com

Mike Holt Enterprises, Inc.
888.NEC.CODE (632.2633) ▪ www.MikeHolt.com ▪ Info@MikeHolt.com

NOTICE TO THE READER

Mike Holt's Business Management Skills Workbook, 2nd Edition

Third Printing: November 2017

Cover Design: Madalina Iordache-Levay
Layout Design and Typesetting: Cathleen Kwas

Copyright © 2013 Charles Michael Holt
ISBN 978-1-932685-25-1

Produced and Printed in the USA

For more information, call 888.NEC.CODE (632.2633), or e-mail Info@MikeHolt.com.

NEC®, NFPA 70®, NFPA 70E®, and *National Electrical Code*® are registered trademarks of the National Fire Protection Association.

This logo is a registered trademark of Mike Holt Enterprises, Inc.

If you are an instructor and would like to request an examination copy of this or other Mike Holt Publications:

**Call: 888.NEC.CODE (632.2633) • Fax: 352.360.0983
E-mail: Info@MikeHolt.com • Visit: www.MikeHolt.com**

You can download a sample PDF of all our publications by visiting www.MikeHolt.com.

I dedicate this book to the
Lord Jesus Christ,
my mentor and teacher.
Proverbs 16:3

"For All Your Electrical Training Needs"

Mike Holt
ENTERPRISES, INC.
888.NEC.CODE (632.2633)

We Care...

Since the day we started our business over 40 years ago, we have been working hard to produce products that get results, and to help individuals in their pursuit of learning more about this exciting industry. I have built my business on the idea that customers come first, and that everyone on my team will do everything they possibly can to take care of you. I want you to know that we value you, and are honored that you have chosen us to be your partner in electrical training.

I believe that you are the future of this industry and that it is you who will make the difference in years to come. My goal is to share with you everything that I know and to encourage you to pursue your education on a continuous basis. That not only will you learn theory, code, calculations or how to pass an exam, but that in the process you will become the expert in the field and the person who others know to trust.

We are dedicated to providing quality electrical training that will help you take your skills to the next level and we genuinely care about you. Thanks for choosing Mike Holt Enterprises for your electrical training needs.

God bless and much success,

Mike Holt

Table of Contents

About the Author

Mike Holt is a business man, an educator, an author, a speaker, software designer and Code expert. His interest in business began in the early 70's when he opened a successful contracting firm. With the skills he gained contracting, he launched his second business, Concepts in Electricity, a school dedicated to teaching electrical contractors. Mike went on to start a software company that specialized in estimating software and eventually brought all of his businesses under the umbrella of Mike Holt Enterprises. This experience in several different types of companies has given him a broad perspective on building a profitable business that is committed to its customers and to quality.

From an early age Mike understood the need for working on your business, not just in your business, in addition to the need for continuous education in order to stay current and competitive. It is that knowledge, coupled with his experience in the field and the running of a profitable business for over 35 years that gives him a unique perspective that provides the foundation for this workbook.

Mike attended the University of Miami's Graduate School for a Masters in Business Administration (MBA). This program gave him the knowledge to take his business to the next level. The skills that he developed throughout all of this experience helped him build one of the most successful business management workshops in the Electrical industry. He has helped thousands of electrical contractors improve their businesses by becoming more effective, focusing on the essentials, improving their management skills and learning effective strategies to grow their business.

Companies across the United States have utilized Mike's services for in-house training and expert advice. His unsurpassed speaking ability has been a source of encouragement to companies and agencies such as ATT, IBM, Boeing, NECA, IAEI, IBEW, ICBO, the U.S. Navy, Grand Coulee Dam, and even the government of Mexico. Mike's appeal lies in his ability to teach a variety of subjects to individuals that have different degrees of expertise and this workbook is an example of how he can help individuals learn regardless of their current knowledge level.

Mike resides in Central Florida, is the father of seven children, and has many outside interests and activities. He is an eight-time National Barefoot Water-Ski Champion (1988, 1999, 2005, 2006, 2007, 2008, 2009 and 2012); he has set many national records and continues to train year-round at a World competition level [www.barefootwaterskier.com].

What sets him apart from many is his commitment to living a balanced lifestyle; he places God first, then family, career, and self.

Special Acknowledgments

First, I want to thank God for my godly wife, Linda, who's always by my side, and my children, Belynda, Melissa, Autumn, Steven, Michael, Meghan, and Brittney. A personal thank you goes to Sarina, my long-time friend and office manager. It's been wonderful working side-by-side with you for over 25 years nurturing this company's growth from its small beginnings.

How to Use This Workbook

The field of **Business Management** encompasses many activities that influence the profitability of your company either directly or indirectly. Many of these activities are interlinked one to the other making separation of individual activities a bit difficult. To facilitate your grasp of the uniqueness of the individual activities of management, this workbook is divided into the following four general subject areas:

- **Chapter 1—Business Management**
- **Chapter 2—Financial Management**
- **Chapter 3—Job Management—(Project)**
- **Chapter 4—Labor Management—(Employees)**
- **Annex—Action Plan**

Only topics unique to each subject area are included so that you may at first develop an understanding of the simpler individual parts. With a fundamental understanding of these under your belt, the integrated nature of business management will be easier to internalize, facilitating a solid understanding of the field of Business Management.

In the course of developing this workbook, it was determined that several topics warrant far greater detail than can be included within the scope of workbooks of this type. Visit www.mikeholt.com/products to see our complete range of products and resources that may help you build your business.

A master table of contents is provided at the beginning of this workbook and each chapter has its own table of contents for easier referencing of material.

To further aid comprehension, as each topic is covered you will be presented with a self-analysis form. The questions on this form will help you develop a list of your individual objectives that lead incrementally to obtaining your goal of improving your business management skills. Complete the worksheet to help you set your goals. Circle the number that best represents the importance to you of this skill; then circle what you believe is the number that best represents your current skill level. The difference between those two numbers is the "Gap." The higher the gap, the more work you need to do on this topic. Writing your answers on each Skill Worksheet will help you to identify specific goals that you want to focus on, and giving it a completion date turns it into an Action Plan.

The Annex introduces you to tools that will help you make your Action Plans into a step-by-step guide to support your business efforts and to keep you focused on your goals. The Business Model Guidelines and the Sample Forms are designed to give you resources to help you to move your business forward. Use them in their entirety, or select what's appropriate for your business practices.

Introduction

This workbook was designed to assist you in improving the skills that will help you build and manage your business more efficiently and will aid in the achievement of what many of you feel is a life-long dream of being in control of your own destiny— of becoming a business manager. Being effective, efficient and productive is not an option in today's world of economic and social globalization, it's a necessity.

As a successful business owner and manager, I can tell you that it is the most difficult and yet rewarding task that I have ever undertaken. Managing perfectly is never accomplished. To achieve even a modest level of success requires that you convert from a doing-type of person to a planning, organizing, staffing, controlling, and remotely directing-type of person, and from undertaking the task yourself to accomplishing the task through others—others who you must begin to recognize are vital to your success. All of these words simply say that you must prepare—and that you must be prepared!

Chapter

Business Management

One of the best definitions of the term **management** is simply **executive skill.** This workbook is about just that—management. Not in the sense of the business school theory of management, but the identification and development of essential skills to become a respected and financially successful manager.

Many individuals are motivated to be self-employed, to be the decision maker, and to have more control over their working lives. For many, this motivation ultimately leads to the start of their own company. Starting your own business results in a greater level of risk but this risk is accompanied by the anticipation of future rewards of owning a successful business. This workbook will aid in the achievement of what many of you feel is that life-long dream. Being effective, efficient and productive is essential to success.

As a manager, it is vitally important that you develop and maintain a sense of objectivity and a willingness to recognize change as an ever-present environmental factor of business activity. Change occurs from within and from the outside of a business. Positive change can be brought about through implementation of your management plan. Action and planning (not reaction to events) must be the order of the day. Receiving candid input from your advisers, the people who have current knowledge of your business, and your employees, can be made a part of the everyday business environment by the use of suggestion and recommendation programs. These programs foster a sense of belonging and being a vital part of the organization.

You need not go it alone. Professional management consultants are readily available to lend an attentive ear, judge options and develop executable business plans for firms of any size or age. Professionals focus on financial performance while seeking competitive advantages through proven management practices.

By studying this workbook, you're taking the first step in identifying key areas that need attention, and of achieving your goals.

For further information on this and other workbooks and DVDs in our product line, please call us toll free at 888.632.2633, e-mail info@mikeholt.com or visit our website at www.MikeHolt.com.

There are two major considerations that must be addressed to be successful in business:

Support: Everyone who wants to be successful needs to have encouragement and positive reinforcement. The support of family and close friends as well as business associates and employees is important. If you do not have a support network, do what you can to develop one. Share opinions and discussions. It's a significant factor in the success of your endeavors.

Continuing Education: Take time to "sharpen the saw." By beginning this study, you have indicated that you possess a vital ingredient, the **willingness to learn.** As a manager, you must keep up. If you stop or slow down, you fall behind. Managers no longer can be satisfied with a high school diploma, a college business degree, or even a master's degree. Today, managers must actively participate in life-long learning to stay competitive.

Attend a short course on accounting, taxes or marketing. Take part in industry specific seminars and workshops. Changes in technology result in changes to every career field, and a continuing commitment to learn and implement new ideas is vital. You must keep up; failure to keep up with current business, social and technological changes has directly been linked to the failure of many companies.

Ask yourself—"What technical skills and certifications have you acquired lately?" Which of these have your competitors acquired? Which of these do your customers seem interested in? Have you even asked? If you don't have the latest skills and let your customers and potential customers know, you're giving business to the competition.

The two factors support and willingness to learn, will take you far in your quest for higher profits and proficiency.

Chapter 1—Business Management
Table of Contents

Advertising and Branding

Advertising is an investment to achieve a marketing goal. It is a paid communication or promotion with the main objective being to create more sales. Advertising is one single component of the marketing process. It is also the single largest expense of most marketing plans. It's the part that involves getting the word out concerning your business or services in ways such as:

- Newspaper and magazine ads
- Direct mail, flyers and brochures
- Point-of-sale promotional items such as refrigerator magnets on service calls, or rulers and pens when you pick up a set of plans
- Billboards & signs; Depending on the highway, you can reach as many as 100,000 prospective customers per day
- Radio and television commercials
- Emails
- Web advertising

Branding is an essential component to the success of your advertising.

- It announces who you are and what you do.
- It confirms your credibility.
- It connects you with your customer.
- It motivates the customer to use your company and services.

Your brand is your promise to the customer. It differentiates you from your competition and tells the customer what they can expect from your services. It should reflect you and who you would like to be perceived as.

Your branding should be able to answer the following questions:

- What is your company's mission?
- What are you selling and to whom?
- What are the features and benefits of your services?
- Who do you want to sell to, and why?
- Develop distinctive logos or color schemes for quick recognition; use them on your business cards, truck painting and jobsite signs. Your trucks, for example, are not simply people and stuff movers, they're mobile advertisements about your company. Keep them all in similar colors and styles with the decals in good shape and the vehicles in good clean condition.

- Update and make your brand current; you don't need a major overhaul, just innovative ways to look new and fresh—you want your brand to stay recognizable. There are numerous websites and free resources on the internet that can give you ideas and direction, including the psychology of color, which colors to use and what they mean to different situations and industries.

Just as your appearance, smile, and even your handshake say a lot about you, so does your advertising and your brand. Sometimes we advertise the wrong message, but we're still advertising. Creating an image across multiple mediums, such as trucks, uniforms, business stationary, signs, and Web and yellow page ads builds and reinforces an image in the consumers' mind.

Invest money in advertising as part of your monthly operating expenses. Don't spend needlessly, but don't try to undercut expenses in a way that directly affects your communication with potential customers and those all-important repeat customers. It consumes valuable limited resources as well as money and time, and should be considered carefully. This business function is essential not only to increase your business, but also to replace customers you lose for various reasons. A common mistake is to reduce advertising when business is slow. Instead, you may need to increase advertising to build up your volume.

Advertising and Branding

Rate Importance	minus	My Skill Level	equals	Gap
1 2 3 4 5 6 7 8 9 10	–	1 2 3 4 5 6 7 8 9 10	=	_____

Things I'm doing right: _____

_____

_____

_____

What goals can I set to improve in this area? _____

_____

_____

_____

Specific steps that I must take to achieve my improvement goals: _____

_____

_____

_____

_____

Action plan: _____

_____

_____

_____

_____

When I want to complete this: _____

_____

Appearance

Your appearance and your actions should convey an impression of prosperity and success. Developing and managing an image creates an air of confidence that will encourage people to do business with you. Your individual reputation along with that of your company is a critical factor in the success of your business. Cultivate a reputation for honesty, fairness and quality products with your customers. A reputation of customer satisfaction can be used to your advantage in establishing a good reputation in the business community.

First impressions are lasting ones. The first contact someone may have with your company is with the person answering the phone. Is he or she polite and cooperative? Do they try to sell your company and its services? It's preferable to have one trained person answer the phone, rather than whoever is available. If you can afford it, hire someone to answer phones, handle reception, and do clerical work in the office. Pay specific attention to the selection of this employee, as they are the first point of human contact many customers have with your firm. That makes the job and the person who does that job very important.

Be sure that everyone in the office knows the way you wish the phone to be answered. Establish a written procedure. The phone should be answered with the person identifying the company name, the name of the individual answering the call, and a phrase such as "how may I help you?" Use closing comments like "thank you for calling" and "I'll get back to you soon." It has been found that if the person speaking smiles while giving his or her message, that smile will come across the phone lines. He or she should also speak clearly and give the caller the time needed to state their reason for calling, so that the call may be transferred to the correct person the first time, not after two or three attempts.

Encourage all of your employees to maintain a professional image even under adverse conditions. When you deal with the public, sometimes things can become a bit unpleasant. Train employees how to respond, and what to do when enough is enough. Make sure that your people know that no one has a right to treat others with disrespect.

Do your business cards, stationary and service trucks instill an impression of quality, professionalism and success? You may not always be able to judge a book by its cover, but branding materials can speak volumes about your business, and about you.

Developing a strong positive image can be aided with mental exercises. There is a theory called "self-fulfilling prophecy." When an individual anticipates performance of a certain caliber, it's likely that they will perform according to those expectations regardless of their skill. If an individual has minimal skills and a less than confident self-perception, and if they don't increase their positive self-perception as the skill level grows, chances are their performance will not be improved. Walk the walk and talk the talk—and, so you see, so shall you be!

Building your own self-image as well as that of your employees will dramatically improve the image the public has of your entire organization. It is worth the effort to concentrate on this area of development. Remember—first you build; then you must maintain. The task is never finished.

Related Topics:
- Business Image and Reputation
- Leadership
- Customers

Appearance

Rate Importance	minus	My Skill Level	equals	Gap
1 2 3 4 5 6 7 8 9 10	–	1 2 3 4 5 6 7 8 9 10	=	_____

Things I'm doing right: _____

_____

_____

What goals can I set to improve in this area? _____

_____

_____

Specific steps that I must take to achieve my improvement goals: _____

_____

_____

_____

Action plan: _____

_____

_____

_____

_____

When I want to complete this: _____

_____

Balance (Life)— All Things in Proportion

Related Topics:

• Time Management

Certainly, your business demands your attention for long-range planning and day-to-day administration; however, don't neglect outside activities that are necessary in order for you to enjoy a balanced life. Schedule time for family activities. Take an active part in social affairs, religious worship, and hobbies. Select activities that develop not only your body but your views and your mind as well. Take time not only to smell the roses but also learn about the individual nutrients of our society's soil. For example, by reading history, you will gain an appreciation that decisions made today contain not only the ingredients of future company evolution, but potential revolution as well.

One of the biggest dangers a business owner faces is allowing his or her work to overshadow all other areas of life. Make no mistake about it, your business will influence your selection of clothes, cars, speech, where you go and even what you read and think about.

Without a good balance between professional time and personal time, you will not be able to develop the effective leadership and management skills that are vital to managerial success.

Balance (Life)—All Things in Proportion

Rate Importance	minus	My Skill Level	equals	Gap
1 2 3 4 5 6 7 8 9 10	–	1 2 3 4 5 6 7 8 9 10	=	_____

Things I'm doing right: _____

_____

_____

_____

What goals can I set to improve in this area? _____

_____

_____

Specific steps that I must take to achieve my improvement goals: _____

_____

_____

_____

_____

Action plan: _____

_____

_____

_____

_____

_____

When I want to complete this: _____

_____

Burnout

A simplistic definition of burnout is that it occurs when you're not having fun. It's indicated by a lack of motivation, a "don't care" attitude. It involves psychological, emotional, and sometimes physical withdrawal from a formerly enjoyable activity. Keep a watchful eye out for signs of "burnout" both in your life and the lives of your family members and employees. This may occur during times of short deadlines and heavy production workloads. It is wise for you and your employees to realize that in situations like this, there is a time when the workload will lessen.

The Dangers of Overworking:

- Do your spouse, children or friends complain that you need to spend more time with them? Do they feel that they are last on the list for your time?
- Do you have many business associates, but few friends?
- Do you work even in nonworking situations?
- Do you work at your play? Is all your recreation as much work as being on the job because you play to win every point, improve your every previous performance, and refuse to take losing lightly?
- Do you feel uncomfortable if you are in a situation where you can't be productive, growing nervous as you wait for things even so minor as a red light to change in traffic?
- Do you think of no-goal-related fun as frivolous?
- Do you let the clock run your life?
- Do you take everything so seriously that you miss or resent humorous comments in a work situation?

Once you recognize the symptoms of burnout, take positive steps to counter its negative effects. Evaluate situations objectively and then formulate and implement solutions. Occasionally, job tasks will need to be totally restructured. Simply rotating assigned tasks may alleviate feelings of boredom or repetition.

A good antidote for burnout is to get involved with outside interests that you find relaxing—exercise, sports, social meetings, club memberships, etc. Get away from business to relax and enhance your creativity. **Protect your free time!** Don't become a workaholic.

Related Topics:
- Balance
- Time
  Management

Burnout

Rate Importance	minus	My Skill Level	equals	Gap
1 2 3 4 5 6 7 8 9 10	−	1 2 3 4 5 6 7 8 9 10	=	_____

Things I'm doing right: _____

_____

_____

What goals can I set to improve in this area? _____

_____

_____

Specific steps that I must take to achieve my improvement goals: _____

_____

_____

_____

Action plan: _____

_____

_____

_____

When I want to complete this: _____

_____

Business Forecasting

As our society changes at what appears to be an accelerating rate, and the need to assess the future grows, the importance of business forecasting increases.

Business forecasting is the process of studying historical performance for the purpose of using the knowledge gained to project future business conditions so that decisions can be made today that will aid in the achievement of established goals.

Some unique individuals still manage businesses by intuitive gut feelings, which are not all that bad if you're good at it—but most of us are not. To be sure, judgment plays a roll in forecasting, but it too has changed. Perhaps the most able of forecasters combine a secret formula of math-modeling skills, tempered with portions of gut feelings, and amended by a dash of seasoned experience.

Since the social and economic world's business operates on changes, so must the business manager's view of these worlds. Many factors have combined to create an organizational environmental climate that is faster moving, more competitive, and more complex than in the past, and promises to be more so in the future.

To improve your forecasting skills, identify the major factors that negatively impact various facets of your business. The following is a list of potential suspects for your consideration:

- Prime interest rates
- New car sales
- New home sales
- Unemployment rates
- Local elementary school enrollment
- Building permits
- Copper futures prices
- The price of oil
- Dow Jones Industrial Average
- Weather forecast

When you've identified the major factors that negatively impact your business, try to understand why. Then identify and study those factors that are business boosters. Once you know the factors that are external sources of influence, you can begin to better seek out the internal factors of influence and achieve the goals that you set for yourself. Ask yourself the following questions:

- How will today's sales impact billings in the next 30 to 180 days?
- How does your accounts payable relate to sales?
- How will the increase in interest rates today impact sales in the next 30 to 120 days?

Business Forecasting

Rate Importance	minus	My Skill Level	equals	Gap
1 2 3 4 5 6 7 8 9 10	–	1 2 3 4 5 6 7 8 9 10	=	_____

Things I'm doing right: _____

_____

_____

What goals can I set to improve in this area? _____

_____

_____

Specific steps that I must take to achieve my improvement goals: _____

_____

_____

_____

Action plan: _____

_____

_____

_____

When I want to complete this: _____

_____

Business Image and Reputation

Without customers you have no business. Focus on customer satisfaction and building your relationships. Endangering this relationship even once by overcharging, shoddy work, cutting corners, not following through on service or promises, or by poor attitude, causes you to lose the confidence and respect of the customer and returning to your original relationship is virtually impossible. Remember that a source of additional business is through customer referral. Don't expect a good recommendation from an unsatisfied customer. Establishing a good business image and reputation is the key.

The definition of the word "image" as it relates to management is *the process of managing the desired visual image communicated to others.* "Visual" is a key and defining word for us. It's a mental impression or record made in the short term and perhaps long-term memory of others. When we use the word "process," we need to ask ourselves what type of control system should be used—an open loop, closed loop or feed forward system.

Open loop. We're saying, in effect, that management knows about the company's image, wants to communicate a good one, but never checks to see how the image is currently. Good intentions are what some of us have lots and lots of.

Closed loop. We're saying that management wants to have a good reputation, checks on the current condition of the image, and is making adjustments to that image (after events occur), and after they have had an impact on the company's image.

Feed forward. Management wants a good image, checks up on that image, makes corrections (not after an event occurs but sees the event coming), and begins to know to make adjustments as the events begin to impact the company's image.

Clearly, good intentions will not do. The best condition is when management looks at the coming events and begins to trim the sail just in time to weather the storm without being blown off course, or having the ship swamped and potentially sunk.

Now that we have some idea of how to best manage image, let's look at various business image-conveying things:

- The location of the company building within the city
- The company facilities
- The building(s), trucks, uniforms
- Print media, billboards, newspapers, flyers, magazines, stationary, business cards, bid documents, etc.
- Electronic media, TV, radio, the Web
- Events, county fairs, team support groups, trade shows, welcome wagons, plant openings, expansions, etc.

We're talking about opportunities to create a mental impression under conditions and in places where we want our company to be associated. Our impressions should be made in areas where we have a vested (or want to have a vested) interest, and opportunities to communicate what we are.

Don't expect everyone in the company to think about the positive presentation of the company's image. We use the word managed—not runs on autopilot! The point is an image will be created. Will it be a managed positive one, or an unmanaged lost-at-sea one?

Having considered that, let's go back up to the second half of the title, the part about "reputation." Reputation is *the current sum total of the specific traits attributed to a company by people.* A company's reputation is produced by the memory impressions retained by society of its perceived actions over time.

Generally, how would you describe the reputation that your firm has with the people who are now and will soon be listed in one of the groups titled "past," as in employees, suppliers, and customers? What would you expect it to be—good, fair, or bad? What may cause (or has caused) your firm to have a less than desirable reputation with each of these groups?

What are the causes of the things that go into the building of a good reputation with anyone over time? Your *integrity* is the foundation of your reputation. This doesn't mean you need to be squeaky clean and have no enemies. What this does mean is you need to move, from this point forward, to keep your integrity as strong as possible.

Planning, organizing, directing and evaluating the management functions must be applied not only to monetary considerations but images and reputations as well. You cannot do it all, and you cannot do it alone. You must have help—the best that you can get! Remember, your goal is to maximize the profit from the sum of your projects, and a bad reputation will prevent you from doing that.

Employee satisfaction will work to your advantage in establishing a good reputation in the business community. How you deal with your employees often dictates how your employees represent your organization. Seek out, entice, obtain, fully utilize and keep the best people you can. You must, if you are to have any hope of succeeding as a manager.

Build your reputation through ability, communication and integrity. A good or even great reputation is priceless; it often opens doors and creates opportunities for us to prove our expertise and excellence. It gives us a step from which to start from above our competition.

Related Topics:
- Image
- Customers

Business Image and Reputation

Rate Importance	minus	My Skill Level	equals	Gap
1 2 3 4 5 6 7 8 9 10	–	1 2 3 4 5 6 7 8 9 10	=	_____

Things I'm doing right: _____

_____

_____

What goals can I set to improve in this area? _____

_____

_____

Specific steps that I must take to achieve my improvement goals: _____

_____

_____

_____

Action plan: _____

_____

_____

_____

When I want to complete this: _____

_____

Change

Methods and techniques that worked in the past may not work today. Awareness of change makes management more innovative but it does require an entire laundry list of abilities. None of these are more important than an organizational mindset that accepts, adopts, implements, and then wholeheartedly executes positive change.

Technological advances occur at rapid and varying rates. This results in methods, materials, tools and even manpower that worked well in the past becoming obsolete by today's standards. Managers must not only be aware of external changes that have an influence upon their organizations, they must be in a position to move their companies in time with these changes.

Changes in business markets and trends towards new technologies can harbor growth and diversification opportunities and increased profit margins. Reluctance to recognize and respond to these changes can create a situation of crisis management.

Wanting to learn and keeping abreast of new developments comes easier than **having** to do it. Your ability to accept initial failures improves your chances of final success. Procrastinating must be overcome—having an undone job or change in the back of your mind increases tension. Read trade publications, join associations, and attend meetings. Become involved and active, and you will also become current and up-to-date.

Management as well as field and office employees must understand the inevitability of change and the necessity to grow with it in order to remain competitive. It's natural for employees to resist change because their thinking tells them it's easier to do things the same way they've always done them. Everyone has his or her own level of resistance to change but if you exercise patience and don't press them, your better employees will come around on their own.

Changes in our economy and society require a different organizational flexibility than that found years ago. A spirit of acceptance of innovative change and the challenges associated with it must exist in those firms that are desirous of being gold medal winners in the economic competition we call business.

Change

Rate Importance	minus	My Skill Level	equals	Gap
1 2 3 4 5 6 7 8 9 10	–	1 2 3 4 5 6 7 8 9 10	=	_____

Things I'm doing right: _____

_____

_____

What goals can I set to improve in this area? _____

_____

_____

Specific steps that I must take to achieve my improvement goals: _____

_____

_____

_____

Action plan: _____

_____

_____

_____

When I want to complete this: _____

_____

Communication

Remember one thing when you're talking with people—to be able to truly communicate, you need to know what the other person means, not just what they say. Did you catch that one? Think about it. It's important in reverse too. You need to make people understand what you really mean.

There are two separate aspects of communication with your employees.

The first is the **mode** of communication with field employees while they are out on the job. If you need to get in touch with someone today, there is an endless selection of outlets to choose from, including email, text, cell phone. An employee can be contacted to take charge of an emergency job or change of schedule, change in plans or specifications, or refrain from making a cancelled call. You need to choose the communication method that works best for your company and establish some rules so that constantly receiving messages while in the field doesn't become bothersome or distracting.

- Establish times during the day (like first thing in the morning and at the end of the day) when you schedule "meetings".
- Always communicate with your employees when there is a change in the job status or conditions.
- Always have your employees communicate with the customer if there is a delay or other change concerning their job.
- Set safety rules regarding talking on the phone or texting while driving. If the contact is important and they are driving, have them pull over to the side of the road to take the call.

The advantages of being in constant communication far override any cost involved in purchasing the equipment or the voice or data plans involved.

The second aspect is the **manner** in which you communicate with your employees. An unhappy or disturbed employee is usually unproductive. Take the time to find out what their problems are. What are their needs? What kind of conflict exists with other employees, their supervisor or management that you can clear up? Often it takes only a sympathetic ear to help an employee get back on track. Let them know you care about and have concerns for them, and not simply that their work has been impacted negatively. This approach helps to make you appear as a genuinely caring person, not as an isolated figure interested in what you can get out of them.

Don't underestimate the importance of communication. It identifies problems or opportunities within a company and is one of the most important parts of your job.

Related Topics:
- Listening & Learning

Communication

Rate Importance	minus	My Skill Level	equals	Gap
1 2 3 4 5 6 7 8 9 10	–	1 2 3 4 5 6 7 8 9 10	=	_____

Things I'm doing right: _____

_____

_____

_____

What goals can I set to improve in this area? _____

_____

_____

_____

Specific steps that I must take to achieve my improvement goals: _____

_____

_____

_____

_____

Action plan: _____

_____

_____

_____

_____

_____

When I want to complete this: _____

Computers and Technology

The mass of paperwork, the space requirements of a filing system, the specialized knowledge a manager needs to compete in the tough business environment all make the use of technology an absolute necessity in business today. Systems come in a wide range of capabilities, speeds, sizes, and prices. Computer software and apps for smart phones and tablets are commonplace for all types of businesses for scheduling, estimating, billing, accounting, and a wide variety of other purposes.

Before the dawn of the information age, electrical contractors relied on three things for success: their trucks, tools, and knowledge of electricity. Although resistant to change in the beginning, most contractors eventually bought into the computer reality, purchasing a few machines to supplement their operations. But change didn't stop there. Soon, the fax machine and two-way radio became staples. Next, the pager and cell phone became necessities. E-mail and the Internet followed, revolutionizing the business world and forever changing the way contractors work.

The growing market of high-tech tools is changing the way electrical contractors do business. Thanks to this technology, today's contractors are breaking new ground in the area of wireless communications, using laptops, smart phones, iPads and tablets, voice recognition systems, bar-coding devices, and digital Web cameras to communicate with their home office and collaborate on projects over the Internet, transforming traditional business of the past into a virtual construction office at home, on the road, in a plane, or in the field.

The Internet is the most influential tool contractors can use to increase communications and become more competitive. Through online project collaboration, contractors reap significant benefits—no more delays from clogged fax machines, missed telephone calls, and communication breakdowns!

Software and apps for smart phones and tablets offer a host of customized features, including contract management, scheduling, spreadsheet functions, Web access, e-mail, and project management capabilities. The digital cameras in the new cell phones and smart phones improve the efficiency of the entire construction process, transferring digital images for editing, storage and easy retrieval.

Regardless of the method contractors choose to access the Web, this kind of connectivity helps to increase project profitability and productivity, enables clear and effective communications, establishes team accountability, reduces the frequency of meetings, and minimizes the risk of litigation by providing detailed, ongoing documentation. Not only does the contractor get jobs done weeks ahead of schedule (which saves them tremendous amounts of money and allows them to bid or negotiate more jobs), it also greatly increases their potential for future income by establishing a reputation for working smarter and faster than the competition.

Small businesses today need this technology as much as larger businesses do. In a small company, the owner has to wear many hats and perform many functions. After a day's work in the field, they often take paperwork home, and spend more hours doing billing, writing checks, and fulfilling the requirements of Federal and State tax returns, as well as local licenses, permits, etc. With the specialty programs that are readily available, an owner can save time and increase accuracy in all office functions including estimating, general ledger, inventory control, purchasing, payroll and billing.

Organizations of almost all economic sizes can benefit from a networked system of desktop PCs. Do some serious investigation about the features of a system before undertaking such an expense to make sure it offers what you need. Just because computer technology is continually changing is no reason to delay the purchase of a suitable system. If you wait until it reaches the highest state of the art, you'll never buy. Be careful of being overwhelmed by wonderful electronics that have short life spans. Each dollar spent must be invested so that it produces a maximum return on your investment.

Anticipate cost associated with continuing education, or on-the-job training. With changes in technology, hardware and software evolutions are going to be necessitating that we all continue to keep up, or at least remain not too far behind.

When selecting technology, you get what you pay for. Research your purchases and research dealers. Know what you need and make your purchase decision accordingly. Just remember— the busier you become, the more likely you are to forget important things. Use commercially available aids to help you become more efficient.

Related Topics:
- Websites and Internet Marketing

Computers and Technology

Rate Importance	minus	My Skill Level	equals	Gap
1 2 3 4 5 6 7 8 9 10	–	1 2 3 4 5 6 7 8 9 10	=	_____

Things I'm doing right: _____

_____

_____

_____

What goals can I set to improve in this area? _____

_____

_____

_____

Specific steps that I must take to achieve my improvement goals: _____

_____

_____

_____

_____

Action plan: _____

_____

_____

_____

_____

_____

When I want to complete this: _____

_____

Confidence and Positive Attitude

Develop and maintain a positive attitude about your ability to be successful and make a profit. Feel that you will accomplish your objectives. Sure, you'll encounter problems in your business, but so will all of your competitors. There are problems and challenges to every endeavor, but remember that everyone else has to overcome their own difficulties. Know that you can cope with and overcome any problems that arise. Don't let your customers intimidate you into doing extra work without charge, or making concessions that will cost you money. Make it a practice to keep your attention on your work. Don't let your mind wander into extraneous matters that have no relationship to the tasks at hand. Welcome adversity as a learning experience in your life. Believe in yourself and your success, and build your desire to succeed, and your expectation to succeed.

We all have "bad" days and "good" days. It happens—but one of the most important things we must learn to do is develop a positive attitude, especially at those times when it seems the most difficult thing to do. Ability, capability, and availability of resources will go far toward making success possible, but without a positive attitude they're wasted, and success (if any) will be incomplete.

When you spend your time and effort in worry, you are feeding negative energy in your life. Think of worry as a belief that you will fail, or the worst thing will happen in any situation. Likewise, faith and a positive attitude are essential to your success. Make a commitment to think positively and give your best effort at all times. Focus on what you have and not on what you lack and maximize your best assets. Be thankful to God for your opportunities and abilities and live a life of thankfulness instead of worry.

Recognize those in your circle of friends and family who are positive and build your networks and support from them. Avoid networking with people whose negative attitudes do not improve your outlook.

The elements to developing this attitude are **belief, desire and expectancy.** A winner **believes** he or she can win no matter what. They never doubt themselves or their abilities. They believe they are worthy and deserve to win. There is an old saying that is applicable here—"As you believe, so shall you be."

Winners always have a burning **desire** to win. Their desire to win is what makes them a winner. To quote another cliché—"A winner never quits and quitters never win." Finally, winners **expect** to win no matter what the conditions are. Fear, while natural, is negative expectancy—expecting not to win. Confidence is positive expectancy—knowing you are going to win.

These three elements cannot be tested or measured. They are all subjective and internal, but they can all work together to help you develop a winning, positive anticipating attitude.

Related Topics:
- Balance
- Self-Confidence
- Stress

Mike Holt's Business Management Skills Workbook

Confidence and Positive Attitude

Rate Importance	minus	My Skill Level	equals	Gap
1 2 3 4 5 6 7 8 9 10	–	1 2 3 4 5 6 7 8 9 10	=	_____

Things I'm doing right: _____

_____

_____

_____

What goals can I set to improve in this area? _____

_____

_____

_____

Specific steps that I must take to achieve my improvement goals: ___

_____

_____

_____

_____

Action plan: _____

_____

_____

_____

_____

_____

When I want to complete this: _____

_____

Conduct

Recognize that you are a respected businessperson, and conduct yourself accordingly. Look, dress and act in a manner that reflects your position as a decision-maker and manager of people. Developing the skills of self-confidence will help you overcome any inhibitions or shyness you may feel. Observe other industry leaders. Notice the way they enter a room or interact with other individuals with assurance and confidence. Meet with them on equal terms, and don't allow customers to overpower you. Let your conduct instill confidence of others in you, which is the key to successful selling and negotiation.

It's not necessary or professional to discuss publicly in the office, any problems or errors that have been made. Corrections, directions, and constructive criticism should be made privately in a conversation between the two people involved. In regard to criticism (whether giving it or receiving it), the way you react to criticism will be remembered more vividly than the argument you present. Raising your voice or using inflammatory language should never be done. These reactions hurt your chance for future communication.

In order to gain respect, management must be competent. Employees and management should share mutual respect. **Be frank, be friendly, and be fair!** Your attitude and the attitude of your staff are reflected to the public. Make sure your firm reflects a positive image.

This involves treating with respect everyone you come into contact with, including the public, inspectors, vendors, customers, etc. Never diminish another for the purpose of making yourself appear more important or successful. Acknowledge that your employees are human and, as such, are capable of error as well as success. Any fool can condemn, and complain—and most fools do! Never make negative comments about your competition. Let them do their own advertising.

Presenting a professional image is an important step in becoming a professional. Remember, appearance is the first thing noticed by customers or visitors to your office. It is important that all employees, especially those in the reception area, dress professionally and present a good overall appearance and conduct.

If you're having difficulty speaking in public, join Toastmasters International or an organization that concentrates on public speaking, or read a book or two about it. As your company grows in size, you'll need to be able to speak well in public, to present your ideas, and to communicate with several people at one time. Fear is a normal emotion when one starts speaking in public— just like it was when you first started to ride a bike!

Act the part, dress the part—conduct yourself with businesslike attitudes, speech, and manners at all times.

Related Topics:
• Image

Conduct

Rate Importance	minus	My Skill Level	equals	Gap
1 2 3 4 5 6 7 8 9 10	–	1 2 3 4 5 6 7 8 9 10	=	_____

Things I'm doing right: _____

_____

_____

_____

What goals can I set to improve in this area? _____

_____

_____

_____

Specific steps that I must take to achieve my improvement goals: _____

_____

_____

_____

_____

Action plan: _____

_____

_____

_____

_____

When I want to complete this: _____

_____

Creative Tension and Personal/Position Power

Creative tension is the primary source from which effective leaders derive their power. One can compare creative tension to a bow and arrow. The bow is nonfunctional as a weapon until tension is applied. When the arrow is placed on the string and pulled, it increases the tension. The potential power of the weapon is then developed. Therefore, the power and effectiveness of the arrow lies in the tension exerted in the bow.

Leaders throughout history derived their influence and power through creative tension, not tension as in destructive stress, but tension as in potential energy—energy to achieve, to accomplish. This creative tension, unique to each leader, exists between love and fear, position power and personal power, success and effectiveness, and the current and the possible. To achieve, we must begin from the current conditions we face today if we are to ever achieve the possible future we hold only in our mental vision.

One form of creative tension exists between the use of love and fear as one leads. Leaders who use only fear to motivate their employees will find it leads to hostility, retaliation and other negative feelings among staff members. Leaders who motivate totally out of love will also be ineffective. A balance must be found. It's best to love one's employees, but use discipline, authority or fear when handling them as the specifics of the situation dictates. Always let your employees feel that you have genuine care and concern about their well being, but that you have the final responsibility for success and failure of the company.

Power in the leadership position can be derived from personal power or position power or a combination of the two. Individuals who are able to derive their power from the loyalty and support of their employees have personal power. Those who are able to induce employees to do a certain job because of their position have position power.

Personal power stems from the following sources:

1. Legitimate influence is the employer's inherent right to lead.
2. Reverent influence is the respect employers receive because of past accomplishments, and usually strengthens over time.
3. Expert influence describes how well employers "know their stuff."

Position power stems primarily from the following two sources:

4. Reward influence is the positive reward the employee believes the employer can provide.
5. Coercive influence is the employee's perception that some type of negative response will follow if they don't comply with the aims of the employer.

Balance the five sources of power in a way you're most comfortable with. Build and develop the sources of power that can work best for you. With time and experience, you'll become more knowledgeable and quickly be able to make decisions that are beneficial for your entire organization.

Another aspect of creative tension is the balance between success and effectiveness. Success denotes actual performance while effectiveness describes the internal satisfaction of an individual employee. For example, if you promote a field employee to a supervisory position and the employee does well, the promotion was successful, but if the employee is not satisfied with the new position, the promotion may prove ineffective and possibly detrimental in the long run.

A good leader must constantly be in the process of trying to be successful (external) and effective (internal). To balance these two factors, keep in mind one important principle—**A good leader must bring together the goals of the employer, employees and the entire organization.**

Creative Tension and Personal/Position Power

Rate Importance	minus	My Skill Level	equals	Gap
1 2 3 4 5 6 7 8 9 10	–	1 2 3 4 5 6 7 8 9 10	=	_____

Things I'm doing right: _____

_____

_____

What goals can I set to improve in this area? _____

_____

_____

Specific steps that I must take to achieve my improvement goals: _____

_____

_____

_____

Action plan: _____

_____

_____

_____

_____

When I want to complete this: _____

Creativity/Innovation

The success of any business depends on a good supply of timely information and owner/manager creativity. Always strive to be one step ahead of the competition by using creative and innovative ideas in your marketing and sales techniques. Research other successful businesses and see the types of advertising and sales techniques that they are using. Modify the ones you like to suit your specific needs.

Innovation commonly occurs in materials, methods, and markets in all types of businesses. The objective of innovation should be the creation of new or increased profit, or result in a reduction in consumption of limited resources or reduction in pollution. Investment in original innovation is the most risky of all investment options since it requires intensive and sustained cutting-edge research. Adapting proven new innovations is much less risky.

Re-innovation is an attempt to extend the life of a given profit center. Prime areas of possible re-innovation are those areas that are approaching a level plateau of maturity in sales, market share and return on investment.

Innovations need not always involve great new scientific discoveries. Many times innovations come from changes in the basics, such as color, ingredients, size or customer perceptions as to the benefits derived from a product or service. Innovations in mature areas can be marginal in nature but major in respect to profit enhancement. Coca Cola was a one-product soft drink maker for many years; now they have several flavors—re-innovations of the original Coke.

Remember that the use of color and graphic design (logos) are easily identifiable by the general public. Take advantage of others' ideas—ask co-workers, friends, associates and family members to help you design a memorable style to be associated with your business. Once your customers learn to associate your company with a specific color or logo, you'll know that you've selected a winning design and you'll want to continue to use it in other communications.

If you have been in business for some time and already have a logo and design that you have been using, be innovative with your layouts and the use of the elements that define your branding so that you are always presenting a current and fresh image while still maintaining your "identity."

Creativity/Innovation

Rate Importance	minus	My Skill Level	equals	Gap
1 2 3 4 5 6 7 8 9 10	–	1 2 3 4 5 6 7 8 9 10	=	_____

Things I'm doing right: _____

_____

_____

What goals can I set to improve in this area? _____

_____

_____

Specific steps that I must take to achieve my improvement goals: _____

_____

_____

_____

Action plan: _____

_____

_____

_____

When I want to complete this: _____

_____

Crisis Management

Crisis Management occurs when there is no control. Effective management is concerned with long-range planning, establishing objectives and developing policies that will carry out these objectives. However, if all of the manager's time is taken up by putting out fires, or reacting and not initiating, then you have an atmosphere of crisis management that retards the growth, expansion and especially the profitability of the company. Crisis management is usually the result of improper planning.

This management method requires one to deal with the most serious problem right now. All other problems take a back seat and are not dealt with until the next major crisis arises. Obviously, there is no control, and no planning. The result is an epidemic growth in negative stress.

To avoid working in an atmosphere of crisis management, pay attention to what you are doing. Learn to set priorities. Delegate effectively and have confidence that the individuals who are assigned to do a task will perform it to the best of their abilities. Creating a daily to-do list, maintaining a status-report, and having a weekly status meeting can help keep projects in order.

Remember:

- Crisis management occurs when there is no planning.
- Know what you have to do and set goals.
- Eliminate tasks that waste time or could be delegated to someone else.
- Know what you have to do, plan your course of action, and do it now!

Crisis management negatively affects all areas of your business from job management to financial management—as well as all areas in between.

Related Topics:
- Problem Solving
- Procrastination

Crisis Management

Rate Importance	minus	My Skill Level	equals	Gap
1 2 3 4 5 6 7 8 9 10	–	1 2 3 4 5 6 7 8 9 10	=	_____

Things I'm doing right: _____

_____

_____

_____

What goals can I set to improve in this area? _____

_____

_____

_____

Specific steps that I must take to achieve my improvement goals: _____

_____

_____

_____

_____

Action plan: _____

_____

_____

_____

_____

_____

When I want to complete this: _____

_____

Customers

A ringing telephone can be music to your ears. Hopefully, it means that potential customers have heard about your services and are eager to learn more. Or, a caller may have an assignment that is right up your alley. But in today's market you cannot sit in your office and wait for the phone to ring.

Many business owners feel that more business is better business. This is not always true. Lately marketers have been spending more time on current customers, re-vamping what customer service really means, and investing more in customer relationship management systems and building teams to improve on communication with customers. The quality and confidence of your customers is more important than the number. Developing positive relationships with potentially repeat customers based upon respect and dutifully earned trust is difficult and slow, but worthy of your efforts.

Successful organizations strive to continually exceed their customer's expectations. The difference between average and excellent organizations is how effectively an organization obtains feedbag from customers, listens to it and acts on it.

- To make customers feel special, set aside some time to treat each one like the center of the universe. By focusing this way, you could save hours of other relationship-building efforts.
- Ask the customer about his/her problems, successes, and plans. Respond to the customer feedback. The more you listen, the more you'll know what kind of work your customer is open to, and what buttons to push to get it—and act on it. Know and exceed the needs of your best customers.
- Improve your "Thank You." Find a way to make your appreciation mean something to the customer.
  - Include a promotion for immediate action
  - Add useful resources
  - Consider mailing a note on special paper instead of sending an email
- A well-designed survey can help you determine what your company delivers and how it can be improved. It also shows that customer that you care about what they think. It can help build loyalty and help you answer concerns in a timely manner.
  - Did you do what you said you would do?
  - Did you do it in a timely manner as seen from the customer's perspective?
  - Did you help the customer feel confident about the service-delivery process?
  - Do you see things from the customer's perspective?

Word-of-Mouth marketing cannot be underestimated. It could mean the difference between failure and survival.

Related topics:
• Advertising and
  Branding
• Marketing

Part of your overall marketing strategy should include the constant search for new good customers, as all businesses lose customers. The sad part is that many times no one knows why a customer went elsewhere.

When dealing with new customers, particularly on jobs that will generate a large sales volume, call for references. You can call past contractors and supply houses to determine the type of customer the individual or company is to work with. Are they cooperative? Do they pay on time? Do they require a significant amount of changes while the work is in progress, etc.?

Customers

Rate Importance	minus	My Skill Level	equals	Gap
1 2 3 4 5 6 7 8 9 10	–	1 2 3 4 5 6 7 8 9 10	=	_____

Things I'm doing right: _____

_____

_____

_____

What goals can I set to improve in this area? _____

_____

_____

_____

Specific steps that I must take to achieve my improvement goals: _____

_____

_____

_____

_____

Action plan: _____

_____

_____

_____

_____

_____

When I want to complete this: _____

_____

Delegation

Delegation is the giving of something to do to another person. It involves explaining his or her own experience in the area, the objectives to be achieved, the resources that are available, and then informing that person that henceforth, he or she has the authority to perform it. It is not telling them how to do it, or standing over them while they do it. It is the means by which the strengths of others are put to best use. If a manager can admit that some employees are superior in some ways to themselves, or that their skills in certain areas are not up to speed, then they can and must delegate. Failure to delegate leads to failure to properly manage others effectively.

Business managers routinely have more responsibilities than time to carry them out. Too often they make the mistake of thinking no one else can make decisions or handle an important task. They are wrong, of course. This attitude does not inspire subordinates to achieve at enhanced levels of performance and hurts the individual manager's performance as well.

Who to delegate to

If you've followed proper hiring methods, you should have confidence in the individuals you chose. Follow the flow of authority in issuing instructions to employees. The manager delegates decisions and policies to the department heads and supervisors. They, in turn, instruct and direct the activities of employees under their supervision. If you've selected supervisors based upon their abilities, you must now have confidence in your own decisions and let them do their jobs as best they can. Accept the fact that they're going to make mistakes, just as you have. If you don't allow them to fail, you'll prohibit them from enjoying the benefits of succeeding.

What to delegate

Generally, the jobs that should be delegated include:

- **All routine tasks.** A lengthy, repetitive assignment should be assigned to a suitably skilled employee. This includes orienting new workers, preparing some reports, and other reoccurring-type tasks. The jobs in this category probably require more skill and discernment abilities than the routine tasks, so they should be assigned to well-chosen subordinates, not routinely given to everyone in the workplace.
- **Tasks Designed to Upgrade Performance.** Some workers might be ready for promotions or additional task assignments. Their skills at routine tasks are high, and the manager thinks they might be ready to develop new skills. By assigning these workers job tasks outside their current skill areas, they are presented with an opportunity to grow within the organization. This kind of delegation is riskier than the others and requires more supervisory monitoring.

Some jobs simply cannot be delegated. If you are uncertain as to which tasks can be delegated and which cannot, review the job description sheets. Those responsibilities listed under your job classification are yours alone. They include planning, supervising, organizing and plotting workflow. They do not include getting the work done.

How to delegate

In order to be able to delegate, you must first take any specific job, train an individual to do that job, and then let go of the responsibility to see that the job is done. If you have ever given the car keys to a teenager, you know how difficult letting go can be, but the key is to know that you have done your part by training them correctly. Communicate publicly your confidence in them. Let them know that you believe they can handle the job and that you are available for consultation if they run into trouble.

It goes without saying that good delegation requires clear communication. Spell out the details, deadlines, and objectives, and why the task must be performed in a specific sequence and manner. If those points are understood, the delegation will prove to be successful. Don't ask for rush jobs, unless they are absolutely necessary, and then explain the reasons behind the hurry. Don't cry wolf when there isn't one!

Delegation does not mean the withdrawal of responsibility and control. You should continue to provide input in a timely fashion, but only when the need arises. When you're delegating, it's okay to include your recommendations, but remember to leave the worker some creative space too. Employees should be able to make some decisions about how the work is to be handled. Monitor the work without appearing to hover over their shoulders

Effective delegation

Good delegation is a method of measurement of performance—for you and the employee performing the task. Effective delegation is one of your most important managerial skills. You can improve morale, increase productivity (your own and others), and ease your job stress—**if** you delegate wisely.

Tips for Delegation:

- Assign low-risk projects first
- Assign priorities and a due date
- Explain the scope and purpose of the project
- Keep tabs on what you delegate
- Let them put their own spin on the project
- Match the person to the skill required
- Provide training
- Recognize the reality of the learning curve

Remember—the more you delegate, the more time you'll have to find new opportunities for your organization, which will increase sales and revenue at the same time.

Related Topics:
- Leadership

Delegation

Rate Importance	minus	My Skill Level	equals	Gap
1 2 3 4 5 6 7 8 9 10	–	1 2 3 4 5 6 7 8 9 10	=	_____

Things I'm doing right: _____

_____

_____

What goals can I set to improve in this area? _____

_____

_____

Specific steps that I must take to achieve my improvement goals: _____

_____

_____

_____

Action plan: _____

_____

_____

_____

When I want to complete this: _____

_____

Goal Setting

A **goal** is defined as "an end one strives to attain." Everyone at some time talks about things they would like to achieve in business or in their personal life. Some are quite ambitious— "I'd like to start my own business and be listed in the Fortune 500." Some are seemingly minor—"I'd like to clean out my desk (or closet) so when I go looking for something, it's there."

There are health-related goals (quit smoking, exercise daily, lose weight); personal goals (be a water-ski champion, increase my bowling average, change my hair color, get a new car); spiritual goals (establish a better relationship with my children, attend religious services on a regular basis); and business goals (get a promotion, a raise, additional training). Setting goals for personal improvement means that you want to improve some aspects of your life.

People have a natural tendency to conform. They listen to their friends, co-workers and associates. Unfortunately, people around you don't always support your goals. They may belittle your aspirations for various reasons. If you're trying to better yourself, perhaps by going back to college, chances are someone is going to make fun of you. Names like "brown-noser," and "goody-two-shoes" are all too common because a few people feel threatened by another's attempt at bettering themselves.

Goal setting is difficult, not only because it forces you to objectively evaluate each goal that you choose to set, but also because it requires extraordinary commitment to follow through and achieve those goals. To achieve success, you must concentrate on becoming result oriented. Have a sense of the mission you are trying to achieve. Assess your own strengths and limitations objectively. Think hard about what you want to achieve and consider any financial resources needed, as well as compromises and sacrifices that may have to be made. Determine if this is something you really want to accomplish—then **DO** it!

Setting your own goals:

The first step is to identify your goals—**right now!** Procrastination is one of the biggest barriers to effective goal setting and requires a strong effort and commitment on your part to make every moment count. Ask yourself questions like:

- What does success mean to me?
- What are the five most important things in my life?
- What do I want to accomplish in my work?

There are basically two types of goals, long-range and short-range.

Make a list of everything you ever considered doing or accomplishing. Your list can include topics ranging from business, financial, family, spiritual, physical or mental goals. Use a "brainstorming" form to write everything that you've ever considered being, doing, or having. List as much as you want. Even "off the wall" goals belong here, because even "off the wall" goals have a basis that may have to be modified, but can be used as a starting point for establishing your own goals.

The next step is to identify what goals you want to accomplish first. You can't reach all of your goals at the same time. Determine if the goal is short-range (can be accomplished in one year or less), intermediate (can be accomplished in one to five years), or a long-range or lifetime goal. Set realistic dates to achieve your goal(s) and write these dates down. Once the list is made, don't put it in a drawer and forget about it. Place the list in your bedroom, perhaps on a mirror, so that you'll look at it everyday. To achieve goals, you must be willing to make the commitment to follow up. Review your goal sheets on a monthly basis, at a minimum. **Work hard! Do it now!**

Next, realistically evaluate your present status in each of the goal areas you've selected. Many times it's difficult to be critically objective about these things. Enlist the help of family, friends and other professionals.

For instance, if one of your goals is to develop a strong understanding of financial areas of your business, seek the advice of your accountant to determine if the records you're now keeping and the billing or collection procedures you've established are effective. Begin to develop a list of the steps you're going to take to achieve your goals.

If your goal is to learn a new sport, enlist the help of a coach or personal trainer to lay the groundwork properly. If you've set a goal to become more tolerant with family and friends, ask them how they perceive your feelings toward them to be. This is no time to "flinch" from criticism. Understand that you are asking a question and you must be willing to receive the answers without responding negatively to the feedback.

From these exchanges, you can better determine where you are and be better able to determine approximately how long it will take you to achieve your goal. Decide if you will require additional formal training or perhaps professional counseling, coaching-type help. Research the methods needed to achieve your goals, and plan your completion date accordingly.

Select at least two goals that you will work on every day. It will be easier to select these goals if you remember that you must answer "yes" to these five questions about each of your goals.

1. Is it really my personal goal?
2. Is it morally right and fair to everyone?
3. If the goal is a short-range step, is it consistent with my long-range or lifetime goals?
4. Can I emotionally commit myself to start and finish the project?
5. Can I see myself achieving this objective?

As a confidence builder, especially if you've never set goals before, select short-range goals you know you can reach (one month to achieve).

Another key decision is to decide whether you should share your goals with others. If they are "give up" goals; that is, give up smoking, cursing, drinking too much, etc., almost everyone will provide you with encouragement for goals of this type, and sharing provides encouragement. Share your goals carefully if they are "go-up" goals; that is, earning a promotion or successfully negotiating an increase in compensation, starting your own business, making the team number one, etc. For lifetime goals, make certain you're committed to the goal before you share this idea with anyone. Communicate with those important to you, and ask for their support in achieving your goals. Once you've achieved some success yourself with these techniques, you can share them with family members, friends or co-workers.

Setting goals for your employees:

Just as managers establish their own goals for growth expansion and profitability of the company, so must they establish goals for their employees. This requires a fine balance of creating a goal that will give incentives for employees to extend themselves beyond their current abilities, but not so remote that reaching it will be beyond their ability to achieve, and thereby create a feeling of frustration and apathy.

Ambitious people typically react favorably to a challenge. Your job is to set attainable goals, provide direction, support and encouragement, and make them feel that you have confidence in their abilities and have faith that they will achieve the goals. When you build a challenge with their agreement, you obtain agreement as to their acceptance of responsibility for achievement. No pain, no gain, so the saying goes, but so too does it follow that no potential loss, no potential benefit. To the risk takers go the rewards!

Setting goals for personal improvement means that you're willing to move forward. Don't let your life be filled with regrets and "if only." Make up your mind to do the things that you truly feel will better your life. If you really want to improve your quality of live, whatever the goal, make the commitment and—**GO** for it!

Related Topics:
- Leadership
- Success and/or Mortality Rate

Goal Setting

Rate Importance	minus	My Skill Level	equals	Gap
1 2 3 4 5 6 7 8 9 10	–	1 2 3 4 5 6 7 8 9 10	=	_____

Things I'm doing right: _____

_____

_____

_____

What goals can I set to improve in this area? _____

_____

_____

_____

Specific steps that I must take to achieve my improvement goals: _____

_____

_____

_____

_____

Action plan: _____

_____

_____

_____

_____

_____

When I want to complete this: _____

_____

Groups and Associations

Many industries have associations comprised of companies actively engaged in transacting business in that field. They typically schedule meetings, trade shows, develop standards, and publish many worthwhile publications. These are prime sources of information about current and future trends and pending legislation relating to business in general and specific industries. A manager must be informed in order to gauge the direction of the industry and to make correct and timely decisions about new trends and new technologies.

Just as the computers in your firm must be networked together to share data, you must also develop a human network of links. By becoming active in various business and social organizations, you'll enhance your own professional reputation, increase your knowledge, and open pathways to your business.

You can start by attending meetings, then volunteering to work on a committee or even head one up. This provides opportunities where you can demonstrate your initiative, cooperative spirit and leadership qualities. Once you've been involved, you can add that to your resume. You are also a high-profile contact for potential customers, but what you really get is a whole set of contacts who remember your hard work and dedication. Don't throw that away!

Be careful that you do not let association membership and attendance take more time than you can afford—both professionally and personally. The rewards of participation should be enough to warrant your continued attendance. If you find that it's causing a problem, reevaluate your association memberships and select those that you derive the most benefit from. Knowing how to and becoming an effective manager of your time is vital to enhancing your productivity.

Never allow external commitments to control your schedule to the detriment of your business or your equally vital private life.

Groups and Associations

Rate Importance	minus	My Skill Level	equals	Gap
1 2 3 4 5 6 7 8 9 10	–	1 2 3 4 5 6 7 8 9 10	=	_____

Things I'm doing right: _____

_____

_____

_____

What goals can I set to improve in this area? _____

_____

_____

_____

Specific steps that I must take to achieve my improvement goals: _____

_____

_____

_____

_____

Action plan: _____

_____

_____

_____

_____

_____

When I want to complete this: _____

_____

Leadership

The ultimate compliment in today's society is to be considered a **leader.** We regard leadership as a quality that bestows power, commands respect, and fosters achievement. Leadership skills must be carefully cultivated over a lifetime.

Leadership is defined as the privilege to have the responsibility to direct the actions of others in carrying out purposes of the organization at varying levels of authority, and with accountability for both successful and failed endeavors. The reality is that leadership is tough, and certainly not a quality that everyone can or should achieve.

The demands of leadership are significant, and impact not only the individual leaders but others as well. Leadership entails sacrifice, dedication, focus, hard work, and long hours, and is often lonely. Leadership puts you in a position of becoming a "visible target." People will often turn against you if your decisions are not to their liking. Other people may agree with you simply by virtue of your position. To be an effective leader, you must develop a thick skin and learn to objectively evaluate not only situations, but also the personalities you encounter on a daily basis.

Employees' attitudes, loyalty and productivity, are influenced by the manager's actions. Set an example they can follow with pride in the company and its management, not only with your employees, but also in your public contacts. We live in a dynamic society. Changes are taking place continuously. Be aware of challenges and opportunities. If you stand still, you'll lose ground to your competitors. Your image is what other people perceive you to be. The reputation and respect that other people have for you make it easier (or more difficult) for you to be an effective and responsible leader. Remember, people like to deal with people they consider their peer, but in whom they have confidence and respect. Image is very important—on the job or off.

Leadership is not easy to explain. The goal of thinking hard about leadership is not to produce great, or charismatic, or even well-known leaders. The signs of outstanding leadership appear primarily among the employees. Are they reaching their potential? Are they learning? Serving? Do they achieve the required results? Do they change with grace? Manage conflict?

Leaders are obligated to provide and maintain momentum and clarity, and focus on the organization's mission. Momentum comes from a clear vision of what the company desires to be. It requires a well-thought-out strategy to achieve that vision and carefully conceived, formulated, and communicated plans. The plan must foster and enable everyone to participate in, and be accountable for, achieving established goals. To maintain this momentum, leaders must allow others to lead them.

Finally, a leader must learn to recognize the signals of impending deterioration. This is based on the theory that all forms of energy tend to deteriorate into lower levels of intensity. The warning signals include:

- There is tension among key people.
- Leading with an attitude of strict business protocol rather than a value attitude that takes into account such things as contribution, spirit, excellence and joy.

- Problem solvers are overwhelmed by a growing number of problem makers.
- When leaders seek to control, rather than guide others toward self-accountability and responsibility.
- When the pressures of day-to-day operations push aside consideration of vision, risk management and long-term planning.
- When people speak of customers as impositions on their time rather than opportunities to serve.

There are twenty basic guidelines for effective leadership. Many of the following topics warrant a complete study on their own; however, the following brief coverage will establish a plan of action you should take in order to achieve your true leadership abilities.

1. Trust is vital. It is essential that you be able to trust your employees. This trust needs to be balanced with a willingness to remove people who have proven that they cannot be trusted to make some tough decisions. Without trust and mutual respect among leaders and employees, an organization will often suffer from a combination of low performance and poor morale.

2. A leader should be a good teacher and communicator. Teaching and leadership go hand-in-hand. The leader must be willing to teach skills, to share insights and experiences, and to work very closely with people to help them mature and be creative. In order to be a good teacher, a leader has to be a good communicator.

3. A leader should rarely be a problem solver. A leader should facilitate problem solving but should let others solve most problems. The psychic reward that an employee gets from actually solving problems is quite important. It builds self-esteem and enhances their ability to do still better in subsequent situations. By being the problem solver of last resort, the leader can help the organization grow and thrive.

4. A leader must have stamina. The demands of leadership are very heavy, and no matter how well an executive may plan his or her schedule, there will be times when the pressures and demands will be oppressive. A physical fitness program can help the executive be prepared for those difficult periods that occur in leadership roles.

5. A leader must manage time well and use it effectively. One of the great faults of American executives is the general failure to discipline their schedules, in-boxes, telephones, travel schedules, and their meetings. Staying busy and working very long hours do not equate with leadership effectiveness.

6. A leader must have technical competence. Leaders must not only understand the major elements of businesses but also keep up with the changes. If the leader has a high level of technical competence, then they should be able to trust their intuition. This combination of competence and intuition can be an extremely powerful tool for a leader.

7. Leaders must not condone incompetence. Leaders must be willing to set high standards, to abide by those standards unwaveringly, and to require their employees to live by those same high standards. Inhibitors to this task drain the organization and its capable leaders of the time, energy, and attention needed to accomplish their mission.

In such circumstances, leaders have a responsibility to the organization to remove those who stand in the way of success. When it's necessary to remove people from key positions, leaders should meet with those individuals personally. The removal should be done with grace, style, and firmness. When you call individuals in to ask them to move on, you should be willing to do so—and not end the meeting until you get to the point. In our highly legalistic society, you must know and abide by the laws relating to employee discharge.

8. Leaders must take care of their people. They should recognize not just the top performers but also the many others who are doing their jobs well. Leaders should *never* ask employees to write their own personal evaluations or effectiveness report; leaders should write those effectiveness reports or personal evaluations and make sure that these are done with care and style. Leaders should recognize outstanding employees, while avoiding the pitfalls of favoritism. Thanking people is an important part of taking care of them, because it's taking care of their psychological health. If you can't think of anything to thank someone for, thank him or her for not creating any more problems for you—as you have more than you want!

9. Leaders must provide vision. Leaders may run an efficient and effective organization, but they do not really serve the long-term interests of that organization unless they plan, set goals, and provide strategic vision. Those leaders who are not visionaries (and many are not) should ensure that they have frequent contact with people who have a talent and an inclination for long-range planning, visionary thinking, and innovation. The best leaders are agents for change, and one of the best ways to ensure that this change is accomplished systematically is through good long-range planning.

10. Leaders must subordinate their ambitions and goals to those of the unit or the institution that they lead. Often, leaders have to subvert their personal ambitions in order to ensure the development and maturation of their organizations. If leaders are too ambitious for the organization, or too ambitious for themselves, they may drive the organization in dysfunctional directions. They become a part of the problem rather than a part of the solution.

11. Leaders must know how to run meetings. Much of a leader's time is spent in meetings. Leaders should know what kind of meetings they are attending; they should establish the ground rules for these meetings; and they should be actively involved in the meetings to make sure they stay on track while allowing individuals ample opportunity to express their views and their disagreements. Finally, leaders should know how to wrap up meetings, to draw conclusions, to set up the time and agenda for the next meeting on the subject, and to direct individuals in the meeting to carry out certain tasks as a result of the decisions that have been made. Leaders also must discontinue meetings that are not serving an important purpose. Meetings should serve to accomplish a specific goal. It's important that meetings have written agendas; those that do not are too easily misdirected.

12. A leader must be a motivator. Leaders cannot individually reach all of their people on a regular basis, so they must count on others to provide needed motivation. Commitment to mission, love of the job and the people, dedication to high standards, frequent reinforcement of the organization's plans and goals, strong incentive and reward programs, and lots of compliments for hard work and high performance are all parts of the vital motivation factor.

13. Leaders must be visible and approachable. Some organizations find the application of the four-hour rule a useful guideline. This guideline recommends that leaders should spend no more than four hours a day in their offices. The rest of the time, they should be out with their people. They should be talking with people engaged in production, and with customers, and directly obtaining their recommendations and comments on problem areas. They should be patting people on the back, making short informal speeches, and handing out awards. They should be traveling widely throughout their spheres of influence, and they should be making contact with other key organizations and influencing personnel to ensure that relationships are enhanced and problem areas identified early. Another facet of being approachable is getting involved in sports, hobbies, etc.

14. Leaders should have a sense of humor. Leaders should let people know that every- day business life is not so formal and intense that you can't sit back occasionally and be amused by what's happening. Humor can be a great reliever of tension. Be relaxed and be humorous with people in a positive manner. Negative humor delivered with an acid tongue, intended to belittle others is unprofessional and counterproductive. Off-color humor should be avoided, since it diminishes the dignity of the leader and the organization.

15. Leaders must be decisive, but patiently decisive. Leaders should listen to all sides before making a decision. A decisive leader is an effective leader; an impulsive leader is rarely effective. However, postponing the decision for many weeks or months is rarely a productive tactic. A non-decision is itself a decision and should be recognized for what it is. Risk-taking is frequently an unavoidable essential and healthy aspect of decision-making. Leaders should understand how to implement decisions. They must ensure that decisions are not only carried out but also carried out faithfully in both substance and spirit. While agreement is not always obtainable, acceptance and willing compliance must be.

16. Leaders should be introspective. Leaders should be able to look at themselves objec- tively and analyze where they've made mistakes, where they've turned people off, and where they've headed down the wrong path.

17. Leaders should be reliable. A leader should be careful about what commitments are made, but once those commitments are firm, nothing short of major health problems or a very serious crisis in business or family matters should alter them. Reliability is something that leaders must have in order to provide stability and strength to organizations. Important elements of reliability are persistence and consistency. Leaders must be willing to be flexible, but consis- tency and persistence are important elements of positive leadership.

18. Leaders should be open-minded. The best leaders are the ones whose minds are never closed and who are eager to view issues from the vantage point perspective of others. Leaders should not change their minds too frequently after a major decision has been made, but if they never reconsider, they are beginning to show a degree of rigidity and inflexibility that can spell trouble for the organization.

19. Leaders should establish and maintain high standards of dignity. When standards of dignity are established and routinely emphasized, everyone can take pride in both the accom- plishments and the stylistic image of the organization. A happy combination of substance and style leads to high performance and morale.

20. Leaders should exude integrity. Leaders should not only talk about integrity, they must "do" integrity. Institutional integrity cannot lie dormant until a crisis occurs; integrity must be ingrained and must be nurtured by the organization from top to bottom. Of all the qualities a leader must have, integrity is the most important.

Related Topics:
- Image
- Management's Role
- Motivation
- Schools of Management Thought

Leadership

Rate Importance	minus	My Skill Level	equals	Gap
1 2 3 4 5 6 7 8 9 10	–	1 2 3 4 5 6 7 8 9 10	=	_____

Things I'm doing right: _____

_____

_____

_____

What goals can I set to improve in this area? _____

_____

_____

_____

Specific steps that I must take to achieve my improvement goals: _____

_____

_____

_____

_____

Action plan: _____

_____

_____

_____

_____

_____

When I want to complete this: _____

_____

Legal

As a business owner, there are many areas concerned with legal affairs that you should have a basic knowledge of. Attorneys possess not only knowledge of the law and the courts, but legal advice as well. Advice can be divided into three types: good, bad, and free. Free legal advice can be worth just what you paid for it. Lawyers (both yours and the other guy's) are expensive. Be prepared before you bring in an attorney; learn a bit about the laws that relate to business.

It is suggested that you enlist the aid of an attorney when preparing contracts and other legal documents. They know the specific words and terms that must be included in order for you to come out on top in a court of law. Ask your advisors for the name of a good attorney, get to know your attorney, and develop a solid business relationship. If you don't have confidence in your attorney's ability to fight for and defend you, then you need to find another one. The following are some basic recommendations relative to legal business affairs:

- Learn the basic requirements of contracts, and the meaning of contract terms, such as: formal, informal, expressed or implied, parties to a contract, compensation, meeting of the minds, breach of contract, oral and written contracts, and valid and voidable contracts. Learn a few of the basic concepts of torts and product liability. Learn some of the basics of constitutional, case and administrative law.
- Know the Mechanic's Lien Law, if it's applicable to your business.
- Investigate and know the requirements for licensing, insurance and permitting as required locally and by the state in which you operate your business. Know the local building codes. Not knowing can be expensive—and not complying can be more expensive.
- Know when to bring your attorney into the loop.
- Ask your attorney to look over a few contracts that you're considering signing, and have them explain what each specific clause means, and what it requires you to do.
- Be sure that your field supervisors have and use job progress diaries, and help them to truly understand why they must use them.
- Develop an intimate understanding of the differences between the law and justice, fairness and equity, contract rights and obligations.

Related Topics:
• Contracts

Legal

Rate Importance	minus	My Skill Level	equals	Gap
1 2 3 4 5 6 7 8 9 10	−	1 2 3 4 5 6 7 8 9 10	=	_____

Things I'm doing right: _____

_____

_____

_____

What goals can I set to improve in this area? _____

_____

_____

_____

Specific steps that I must take to achieve my improvement goals: ___

_____

_____

_____

_____

Action plan: _____

_____

_____

_____

_____

_____

When I want to complete this: _____

_____

Listening and Learning

It is important to develop good communication skills. As a manager, you must be able to congratulate, console, confront, motivate, and teach your employees in a variety of ways that will increase their learning and solidify your relationship with the entire organization. There are two "secrets" to effective communication:

- Listen closely to people when they are speaking.
- Notice their individual differences.

The value of listening cannot be underestimated. Good listening is a skill that requires practice. It does not come naturally. Don't try to formulate your answer while the question is still being asked. Wait and pay attention. When advantageous, ask them to please restate a portion of their case. This shows that you are truly considering what they have to say.

Talk to your employees and customers frequently to learn information about your company and find out what's really going on in the process. Observing them regularly will help you become familiar with their communication style, individual mannerisms, and their body language. Being alert and respectful to cultural differences is especially important here. Managers who listen well set a positive example for their employees and provide a foundation for a strong relationship. "A mind is like a parachute—it works best when it is open!"

Just as everyone tends to communicate differently, learning styles are often unique too. In order to improve learning, it's essential that you be aware of each individual's learning preferences. This requires some degree of sensitivity to others and the ability to effectively use different presentation methods.

Some individuals may learn best by having a manager communicate information verbally in a step-by-step manner, while others might learn best by observing the manager demonstrating it. Finally, some individuals may learn best by experimenting on their own without interference of a manager's demonstration or verbal instruction. You can begin to recognize these differences by listening and observing responses to your attempts at communication. "I hear, and I imagine; I see, and I understand; I do, and I remember forever!"

The challenge is for you to communicate with respect to each individual's learning style. The employees often reciprocate this respect as they pay closer attention to what you are communicating. As a result, the employer-employee relationship grows stronger and the likelihood of success within your organization is expanded. Remember—your success is dependent upon your ability to get others to do as you desire.

Related Topics:
- Communication

Listening and Learning

Rate Importance	minus	My Skill Level	equals	Gap
1 2 3 4 5 6 7 8 9 10	–	1 2 3 4 5 6 7 8 9 10	=	_____

Things I'm doing right: _____

_____

_____

_____

What goals can I set to improve in this area? _____

_____

_____

_____

Specific steps that I must take to achieve my improvement goals: _____

_____

_____

_____

_____

Action plan: _____

_____

_____

_____

_____

_____

When I want to complete this: _____

_____

Management's Role

Most people have weak *management skills,* regardless of their position or title. How well do you manage work processes and time? You need to keep up, read about management, attend management seminars, look at best practices, and take some courses. Get new management skills and document them for your resume.

Managers must undertake long-range planning to achieve their goals and growth expectations, and short-range planning to keep busy, pay the bills, and build up financial reserves.

- Know your objectives (what you want to achieve).
- Establish your policies (how you're going to achieve it).
- Decide how you want to position yourself and chase only that kind of work.

In all your planning, recognize the time value of money for it's the fuel that keeps things moving, and the stalling effects that a lack of money can cause. Cash is king—you're out of business the day you cannot make payroll.

Seek your level of competition. Some large firms have evolved to be very efficient and specialized. These firms tend to dominate certain types of construction, so choose your own field of battle. Determine the types of jobs where you have a competitive advantage, and then assign specific resources to obtaining this type of work.

Take an inventory of your tangible and intangible assets. How qualified are your field personnel, supervisors, estimators, sales people and office staff? Are they directed and motivated for maximum productivity? What kind of work can you compete for successfully and make a profit?

All of these words simply say that you must prepare, and that you must be prepared. Being effective, efficient and productive is not an option in today's business world, it is essential.

Management's Role

Rate Importance	minus	My Skill Level	equals	Gap
1 2 3 4 5 6 7 8 9 10	–	1 2 3 4 5 6 7 8 9 10	=	_____

Things I'm doing right: _____

_____

_____

_____

What goals can I set to improve in this area? _____

_____

_____

_____

Specific steps that I must take to achieve my improvement goals: _____

_____

_____

_____

_____

Action plan: _____

_____

_____

_____

_____

_____

When I want to complete this: _____

_____

Marketing

Marketing is the systematic progressive process of planning, implementing and controlling a mix of activities intended to bring you business. It encompasses your research, your advertising, sales, public relations, and customer service and satisfaction. The goal of marketing magic is to communicate your message and boost your business revenue. And you must do that actively. Passively doing a good job and hoping for a good word-of-mouth referral is a good way to give up top line revenue, as well as a good chance at high-margin work.

All too often, a firm's marketing plan is nothing more than who their salesmen and saleswomen will be calling upon next week. Their roles are understood as the task of picking up plans and turning in on time a bid on a plan and specifications job. In turn, price-cutting is seen as a negotiation, where the same job that was originally bid is finally sold at a lower price. Then, the salesperson is given a commission for selling the job at a potential if not preordained loss!

Selling is (for sure) a vital function, but it's only one part of a firm's total marketing plan. Selling does not encompass the entire marketing concept. Marketing can be divided into five tasks as follows:

- Define the market area.
- Research consumer needs.
- Develop products to meet consumer demand.
- Recruit, select, and train necessary manpower to deliver the product, and
- Develop its sales approach and advertising support.

There are three markets that a company may attempt to sell to: general consumers, industrial markets, and governmental markets. Within these markets are various segments with discernible unique needs. Examples are:

- Industrial design and build
- Industrial plan and specification
- Planned service/maintenance
- Emergency repairs

Ask yourself these questions:

- What specific markets does your firm currently sell to?
- What market segments within these markets does your firm currently market to?
- What markets does your firm want to do more (or less) business in?
- What major marketing changes will your firm be implementing next year?
- How are you communicating to this market?

- What strategies do you have in place that will actively increase sales for next week, next month, or next year?

The other decision you will need to make is which avenues to include in your marketing efforts. Social media is the collective name given to a group of internet-based applications that are used to turn communication into interactive dialog between organizations, communities and individuals. The scope and reach is huge, and is growing every day.

Do your research (many free resources on the web) and become knowledgeable about the marketing possibilities available through social media and decide which are right for your business. You can't afford not to stay "connected," so make sure that you have the personnel dedicated and available to post, follow, tweet and keep current.

Don't waste your valuable sales time. Be selective. Target your efforts where you'll have the best chance of getting the business you want at a fair profit.

Related Topics:
- Advertising and Branding
- Websites and Internet Marketing

Marketing

Rate Importance	minus	My Skill Level	equals	Gap
1 2 3 4 5 6 7 8 9 10	–	1 2 3 4 5 6 7 8 9 10	=	_____

Things I'm doing right: _____

_____

_____

What goals can I set to improve in this area? _____

_____

_____

Specific steps that I must take to achieve my improvement goals: _____

_____

_____

_____

Action plan: _____

_____

_____

_____

_____

When I want to complete this: _____

_____

Mistakes

We all make them—mistakes! Many times mistakes make us appear foolish or incompetent. There are two psychological strategies to deal with mistakes:

- Limit focus on the mistake
- Create a positive mental setting for the remainder of your tasks

Limiting focus on the mistake means setting the mistake aside mentally. Once the mistake has been made, there's no way to relive the event successfully. Going over the mistake again and again only rehearses making the mistake. Reviewing the mistake can also lead to self-directed anger or embarrassment. Any thought about the mistake should focus on the technical and controllable aspects of performance, but even this evaluation should only focus on how to correct the mistake and what to do the next time out.

Whether the mistake is yours or an employee's, don't aggravate the issue by asking: "Why did you do such a stupid thing?" but rather ask, "How can we correct this error?"

To create a positive mental setting after making a mistake, identify and focus on technical aspects of the performance that are associated with good performance. This "positive set" needs to include an emotional component, a feeling that "we can do it." Thinking of past successes can generate this feeling.

A failure must be seen as something that has happened and is gone. File it away immediately. If further analysis is necessary, it should be done in the future, after the immediate negative impacts have lost their edge.

The "blame" for a mistake should always be focused on a controllable technical aspect of performance (you did not follow company policy) rather than a weakness in an individual (you're not smart enough). Many individuals are not willing to accept responsibility for a mistake and tend to focus attention or "blame" on co-workers, possibly erroneously. Be open-minded about mistakes and realize that mistakes are going to happen.

We all have "bad" days and "good" days. It happens—but one of the most important things we must learn to do is develop a positive attitude, especially at those times when it seems the most difficult thing to do. With a positive focus, the employee is given something to do to avoid the mistake and is given a feeling that they've been successful many times before—and will be again!

No one really intends to go out and make mistakes. They sometimes are caused by a lack of correct information. No matter how hard one may try, or how well planned a process may be, people are human, errors are made, and consequences exist. Think of mistakes as an opportunity to LEARN.

Related Topics:
- Problem Solving

Mistakes

Rate Importance	minus	My Skill Level	equals	Gap
1 2 3 4 5 6 7 8 9 10	–	1 2 3 4 5 6 7 8 9 10	=	_____

Things I'm doing right: _____

_____

_____

_____

What goals can I set to improve in this area? _____

_____

_____

_____

Specific steps that I must take to achieve my improvement goals: _____

_____

_____

_____

_____

Action plan: _____

_____

_____

_____

_____

_____

When I want to complete this: _____

Motivation

In order to motivate your employees, you need to first be motivated yourself. You need to have a firm understanding of where you want the job to go, be aggressive about doing it, and excited about taking on the challenge. Then you must communicate these feelings to your employees. Your job is to lift your employees out of mediocrity and make them achievers.

Motivation is extremely important. Non-motivated employees can have several negative effects on your business. These include an adverse effect on the customer, friction on the job, substandard output in quality, a high turnover of employees, absenteeism, tardiness, and many of the disciplinary problems that you wish to avoid. It is a fact that motivated employees are the most productive and will produce to their maximum abilities.

To bring about a positive change in behavior, management needs to be aware of and deal with the different motives employees have for performing their jobs. This is the most critical ingredient to a successful motivation formula. Managers should provide the availability for achievement, manipulate the expectancy for success, and take into consideration the incentives for action, which differ from individual to individual.

Recognize that there are dangers in the use of external pressure to perform. Excessive incitement to pressure often hampers the performance level. The process of motivation is not concluded with any one particular performance, but rather is constantly reassessed as new information is obtained through practice and continued work. Results have to be placed in perspective so that the individual realistically evaluates successes and failures.

Carefully analyze the performance of individuals and provide each with attainable personal goals. Concentrate on the specific elements of an individual's performance and reward on the basis of achieving personal goal increases. This will keep morale high. Stress the attainment of small goals. Employees can then build on their accomplishments. Keep written documentation to help identify problems that may go unnoticed, as well as achievements and improvements. Look for gradual gains. Know your individual employees. What motivates one specific individual may have no effect on another. Any motivational strategy you use should have realistic and attainable goals the whole organization can strive for.

Practice and teach self-reinforcement. There are two steps to this process. Nurture an understanding in your employees of their own physical, technical and mental attributes. In other words, make them aware of the strengths and weaknesses in their abilities. Establish two-way communication. Instead of telling employees what they did wrong and telling them to correct it, ask them what they thought they did wrong, and what they would do to correct it next time.

In addition to making individuals aware of different aspects of their performance, it enables them to make objective evaluations of their own performance. Two-way communication also provides for better and more specific feedback, which enables individuals to improve more quickly.

Related Topics:
- Goal Setting
- Leadership

Motivating individuals is not a simple task. It's very difficult and requires significant skill to execute fairly. If you're not sincere, others will sense it. If you lack genuine care for others, it will be uncovered. If you are manipulative, you will anger others. Some people can coach; some can lead; yet others (a few others) can do both. Know your own limits.

The operation of a business is a team task; so too is management. If you're not a good motivator, delegate the task to others. The ability to motivate others is important. Words are cheaper than dollars; you cannot continually throw dollars at people hoping to properly motivate them.

Motivation

Rate Importance	minus	My Skill Level	equals	Gap
1 2 3 4 5 6 7 8 9 10	–	1 2 3 4 5 6 7 8 9 10	=	_____

Things I'm doing right: _____

_____

_____

_____

What goals can I set to improve in this area? _____

_____

_____

_____

Specific steps that I must take to achieve my improvement goals: _____

_____

_____

_____

_____

Action plan: _____

_____

_____

_____

_____

When I want to complete this: _____

_____

"No"—The Most Difficult Word

When you're getting started in business, you'll feel you must bid on every job that comes along. This is natural and it's okay. This gives you plenty of opportunities to practice your estimating skills. However, if you provide your customers with a quality job at a fair price, you'll become busy and will need to be selective of the jobs you bid on.

Don't say "yes" or "maybe" when you want to say "no." Be assertive, not deceptive. Don't accept a job that won't let you recover your cost, or take on responsibility when you have no obligation. Resistance to sales efforts by others may not come easy, but don't let yourself be talked into doing anything that is contrary to your company's best interests. Say "no" and mean it!

Although it may be difficult at first, with practice you'll find it easier to draw the line tactfully and protect your time. Said correctly, people usually respond well to a "no." It requires clear, logical thinking. Don't be wishy-washy!

You can reduce your aggravation level by saying "no" to a situation you cannot handle, or don't choose to handle.

Be realistic when making a schedule. Consider what you're actually able to do versus what you would like to do. There is nothing wrong with saying "no" if you know that added responsibility will cause a serious problem with your schedule. A survey suggested that if you were to say "no," your answer would be correct 80 percent of the time.

Is there a right time to refuse a business opportunity? Even if you have to turn down potential customers, you don't want to close the door on the possibility of working with them in the future. Whatever you decide to do, be honest with your customers. Explain why you can't take on the project and provide realistic assessments of the alternatives. If you do refer them to another source, make sure that business is as qualified as you are. Your customers will appreciate your good advice, and be more likely to solicit your help again in the future.

"No"—The Most Difficult Word

Rate Importance	minus	My Skill Level	equals	Gap
1 2 3 4 5 6 7 8 9 10	–	1 2 3 4 5 6 7 8 9 10	=	_____

Things I'm doing right: _____

_____

_____

_____

What goals can I set to improve in this area? _____

_____

_____

_____

Specific steps that I must take to achieve my improvement goals: _____

_____

_____

_____

_____

Action plan: _____

_____

_____

_____

_____

When I want to complete this: _____

Peer Pressure

Peer pressure is not only a problem for the young. The term peer pressure is often used by parents who are concerned about their children following the example of the "wrong" type of crowd, particularly in the use of drugs. But, it isn't just affecting children.

Don't be affected by what other people do or feel unless it's something you agree with. For instance, if you're an electrical contractor, don't do commercial work if you prefer residential, merely because "everyone" says you can't make money doing it. You can't get ahead that way.

It's unfortunate but true—people like to make others feel stupid. Putting someone down is somehow easier than building another up emotionally. Many people often give opinions and recommendations without knowing the facts. And, sadly, people don't like to see other people become successful.

Everyone wants to feel accepted and, unfortunately, many times we adjust our behavior and attitudes to match those of the majority, giving little consideration to our own basic feelings. This certainly increases the stress level of individuals.

Assess your own strengths and limitations objectively. Make your decisions and perform your activities based on your own knowledge and ability. If you elect to receive advice and opinions, do so with an open mind. A bit of old-time wisdom fits in here very appropriately—"To thine own self be true." Usually, you can't go wrong!

Peer Pressure

Rate Importance	minus	My Skill Level	equals	Gap
1 2 3 4 5 6 7 8 9 10	–	1 2 3 4 5 6 7 8 9 10	=	_____

Things I'm doing right: _____

_____

_____

_____

What goals can I set to improve in this area? _____

_____

_____

_____

Specific steps that I must take to achieve my improvement goals: _____

_____

_____

_____

_____

Action plan: _____

_____

_____

_____

_____

When I want to complete this: _____

_____

Planning and Organizing

Keeping yourself organized is the only way that you're going to get everything done effectively. There are two basic rules to follow—write it down and review all of your notes at least once daily.

Let's face it. If we don't write things down, almost all of us will forget to do something. Our schedules are just too busy and there are just too many things to be done. How many times have you gotten yourself in a sticky situation because you forgot about something? If you're like most people, it's been quite a few times.

Once you've made your plans and lists, cross out those things that are done. Carry items not finished to the next day. Eliminate items no longer needed. If at all possible, only handle a piece of paper once. Look at every action you take and determine if it's assisting you in obtaining your goals. If not, don't do it!

The biggest time-waster is not being able to find information that you need when you need it. Some managers use a day-desk away from their office upon which nothing remains when they leave. The incoming mail and correspondence are processed and assigned to others each day. This allows the executive to determine what comes to them, and what is assigned to others. It provides them with timely and unfiltered access to written communications with the company, and to know first-hand what bills and checks have come in, along with other important documents. It also allows them to delegate the task of providing responses to others. A manager should:

- Set objectives and deadlines.
- Delegate responsibility and accountability.
- Utilize commercially available organizers, such as smart phones or tablets to help make better use of your time.
- Determine once a year what national and local activities you can and will participate in, and do the same for local business, social, and religious activities. This gives you a good idea of how limited your time really is.

Related Topics:
• Time Management
• Leadership
• Problem Solving

Resolve schedule conflicts as early as possible. If you have something to do and can't get it done, plan to complete it the next day or at the next available opportunity. Never allow one missed appointment to cause a delay for the remainder of the day. Apologize, reschedule, and continue through the day.

Organize your time and plan wisely. One of the great faults of American executives is the general failure to discipline their schedules, in-boxes, telephones, travel schedules, and their meetings. Staying busy and working very long hours do not equate with leadership effectiveness.

Planning and Organizing

Rate Importance	minus	My Skill Level	equals	Gap
1 2 3 4 5 6 7 8 9 10	–	1 2 3 4 5 6 7 8 9 10	=	_____

Things I'm doing right: _____

_____

_____

_____

What goals can I set to improve in this area? _____

_____

_____

_____

Specific steps that I must take to achieve my improvement goals: _____

_____

_____

_____

_____

Action plan: _____

_____

_____

_____

_____

When I want to complete this: _____

_____

Problem Solving

We encounter problems every day—at home and at work, with our families and our associates. And we spend a tremendous amount of time and energy trying to solve them. Many times we find that we haven't! There is a theory called **"breakthrough thinking,"** which is an approach to planning and problem solving based on scientific theories and years of research. It begins by defining our purpose in solving a problem, rather than focusing on what is wrong in a situation.

Breakthrough thinking assumes that the world is always in a state of flux. Each solution creates a new problem (today becomes history, the future becomes today). No matter how similar the problems may appear on the surface, no one solution can work all the time or for all things. To take advantage of these ever-changing conditions, this process always seeks out the **solution-after-next.** As a result, it represents a process rather than a fixed goal—a flexible plan to achieve what matters most to us. The process is founded upon the following basic principles:

- **The Solution-After-Next Principle.** Innovation can be stimulated and solutions made more effective by working backward from an ideal target solution.

- **The Uniqueness Principle.** Each problem is unique and requires a different approach. Although no two situations are alike, most people rely on impulsive idea-borrowing to solve their problems.

Problem solvers who accept differences are much more likely to be successful than those who see only similarities, and who try to shoehorn borrowed solutions into situations where they are not appropriate. When the only tool you have is a hammer, all problems tend to look like nails.

- **The Purposes Principle.** Focusing on purposes helps strip away nonessential aspects to avoid working on the wrong problem.

In applying this principle, for example, a job seeker might accept a lower salary at a growing firm with strong opportunities for advancement, rather than a higher salary in a dead-end job at a small family firm. The key question is not "what is best for me next week," but "what do I want to be doing five years from now?"

- **The Systems Principle.** Every problem is part of a larger system. Nothing exists by itself. Successful problem solving (and problem prevention) takes into account these interrelationships between many elements and dimensions.

- **The Limited Information Collection Principle.** Knowing too much about a problem initially can prevent you from seeing some excellent alternative solutions.

Information junkies think that facts are the keys to problem solving, and that the more facts you have, the better your solution will be. They fail to realize that facts are only static representations of the real world, not the real world itself. Representations can be distorted, poorly interpreted, irrelevant (the wrong problem) or just plain wrong. Even if they are accurate, a flurry of facts will obscure the primary problem-solving factor in any good solution—the purpose for it.

- **The People Design Principle.** The people who will carry out and use a solution must work together to develop the solution. A perfectly designed plan poorly executed will fail. An imperfectly designed plan perfectly executed will succeed.

Too many meetings end up being attempts to assign blame. Because they focus on the particulars of a problem, participants take turns in pointing fingers at someone else. **Alternative:** At the beginning of the meeting, ask everyone to discuss the purpose of your getting together. When individuals feel free to express their needs, they become more useful (and less defensive) contributors.

- **The Betterment Timeline Principle.** A sequence of purpose-directed solutions will lead to a better future.

Breakthroughs often occur over a period of time, not just at one point. The easy, foolproof solution is usually a patch job—and it's almost always wrong. Since solutions are changes that include the seeds of later changes, this principle demands continual improvement in the area of concern. Traditional thinkers say, "if it isn't broken, don't fix it!" But breakthrough thinkers say, "Fix it **before** it breaks!"

In spite of the most careful planning, it is impossible to anticipate every problem. You can't accurately predict long-range weather, sickness, business conditions, or financial security of your customers. So, when a problem shows up, make sure you understand the facts in order to attack it directly. Dealing with the side effects or secondary impacts will not remove the problem. Covering up for an employee who is often late or absent without cause is only a temporary solution. Find out why, and take a course of action. The longer the noxious weed is allowed to grow, the deeper the roots, and the more difficult it is to remove.

On occasion, there will be no clear-cut solution. In such cases, when you recommend action, have an alternative plan in mind to be used in case of failure. I have a technique that I use with my employees that seems to work very well because it not only reduces my problem-solving responsibilities, it instills greater confidence in problem solving for them. I tell them—"Don't bring me problems, bring me solutions! I have more than enough problems—what I need are solutions for the ones I already have!"

Related Topics:
- Planning and Organizing
- Leadership
- Mistakes
- Time Management

Problem Solving

Rate Importance	minus	My Skill Level	equals	Gap
1 2 3 4 5 6 7 8 9 10	–	1 2 3 4 5 6 7 8 9 10	=	_____

Things I'm doing right: _____

_____

_____

_____

What goals can I set to improve in this area? _____

_____

_____

_____

Specific steps that I must take to achieve my improvement goals: _____

_____

_____

_____

_____

Action plan: _____

_____

_____

_____

_____

When I want to complete this: _____

_____

Procrastination

Procrastinate—The definition of the word procrastinate is to put off doing until a future time, to postpone habitually, or to delay needlessly.

Preventing Procrastination—The following reasons for procrastination will no longer be a problem if you identify them and deal directly with them realistically:

- **Perfectionism**—Some people have impossibly high standards. In this situation, we're all likely to put off what we fear cannot be accomplished. Therefore, think **performance,** not absolute **perfection.** Set manageable, concrete incremental goals to be accomplished at specified times.
- **Large Overwhelming Tasks**—When what you are doing seems so large and complex you don't know where to start, procrastination often results. In a situation like this, break the work into manageable units that will take you no more than ten to thirty minutes each. Take one small step at a time. Build upon success.
- **Unpleasant Tasks**—If you hate doing something, you're likely to put off addressing it. When possible, delegate or hire someone to do the tasks that are most hateful to you. If you must do them yourself, think about how good you'll feel when the task you've been avoiding is done. Also, use the tactic of doing unpleasant tasks first to get them out of the way and free the rest of your day to pursue more pleasant tasks. You may also decide that you are **NOT** going to do something.
- **Creating Pressure to Perform**—Some people motivate themselves by creating the pressure of a crisis atmosphere. They procrastinate until the last minute and then dramatically complete the work. Since this strategy actually helps them get the work done, they're often confirmed procrastinators. The emotional expense, however, is great and detracts from the kind of consistent, concentrated effort a successful business needs. So instead, motivate yourself by working at a reasonable pace to finish one step at a time rather than working yourself into a panic to do it all in one last-ditch effort.

Sometimes procrastination is a warning signal, a way to tell you that this is not the right thing to do or that it is a waste of time and doesn't need doing. When, for whatever reason, you find that you continue to avoid important tasks, identify what you're doing instead, and cut off your escape routes. If you chronically procrastinate and find you can't cut off the escape routes, ask yourself the following questions:

Under what circumstances would you be motivated to do what needs to be done?

Listen carefully to your answer. Don't try to modify it. Think about what's stopping you from going on with what you need to do. If you're honest with yourself, you may recognize that you're not willing to work as long or hard as it takes to get the job done. You may not have scheduled enough free time for yourself. You may not be willing to do some of the tasks your work entails. In any case, now you have to face the truth because you are the boss. If you're unable to solve your own problems, to manage yourself, what will your future hold?

Do you enjoy your work?

If the honest answer is "no," it's no wonder you're having difficulty getting yourself to do the tasks involved. If you really don't like your work, seriously consider finding different work.

Some ways to address procrastination:

- Break the task into small manageable pieces.
- Do the hardest part first.
- Don't worry about being perfect.
- Give yourself a deadline.
- Reward yourself when you complete the task.
- Set a fixed time to work on it.

One last word of advice—**protect your free time!** Everyone needs to take time for relaxation and having fun. Engage in hobbies or other pursuits that you enjoy. Don't become a workaholic.

Related Topics:
- Time Management
- Problem Solving
- Motivation

Procrastination

Rate Importance	minus	My Skill Level	equals	Gap
1 2 3 4 5 6 7 8 9 10	–	1 2 3 4 5 6 7 8 9 10	=	_____

Things I'm doing right: _____

_____

_____

_____

What goals can I set to improve in this area? _____

_____

_____

_____

Specific steps that I must take to achieve my improvement goals: _____

_____

_____

_____

_____

Action plan: _____

_____

_____

_____

_____

_____

When I want to complete this: _____

_____

Reading

The first thing you received when you decided to take a leadership course, or business management course, or almost any other course, was a manual. Is your home or office a mountain of letters, memos, magazines, and books—waiting for you to sort through and read? It looks hopeless, doesn't it? Many of us have a first inclination to throw it all out—it takes less time and certainly would eliminate the "mountain" but, on the other hand, a lot of the information in that pile is going to provide us data we need to perform effectively.

There is more information in even a highly specialized field than any one person can keep up with. To better manage the time you spend reading without losing out on vital information, skim the table of contents, directories, and headlines. Read only pertinent material in depth. Learn to read more quickly by taking a speed-reading course. Have someone in your office clip articles that are pertinent to your needs and interests. Establish a management reading file that is passed around each month to key personnel.

For most of us, reading is an important aspect of learning about new developments and catching up on what is going on in our professions. If you are about to tackle that mountain (or are trying to avoid it altogether), here are a few helpful suggestions to better manage what you read:

- Develop a list of books, magazines and newspapers that you want to read, and read those sources first. Set goals and reasons for reading each information source. Establish a yearlong reading plan, and then follow your plan. Read with a purpose.
- Eliminate everything you really don't need to read. This not only helps to save time, but it makes the piles look smaller, which is encouraging.
- Cancel subscriptions to magazines you don't need—it saves you money and time. Get off mailing lists for information that's not necessary or enjoyable for you to read. Yes, enjoyable! Be sure to take some time in your day to relax and pursue your own interests.
- Keep a constant check of what you read and evaluate its importance to you. If you don't need it, pass it on to others who may benefit from it, or just throw it away.
- Put deadlines on your reading materials. If you haven't read those magazines in over two months, you probably never will—throw them out!
- Keep a file folder of articles you want to re-read or refer to. Just tear out what you need, rather than keeping the entire magazine. Learn to skim over these and other reports, circling the important ideas to remember.
- Take your reading on the road. Set up a reading folder that is portable so that you can read prior to appointments, or in doctor's offices, etc. Better yet, purchase an electronic book reader and download your books or magazines.

- If there is information on a topic that you need, go to the web, search for that topic and read what you need to know online without purchasing and storing unnecessary publications.
- If there is a particular topic that you would like to be informed about, set up a Google Alert for your email account. You can enter a subject or topic you want to be current on, and every day you'll get an automatically generated email with a list of all relevant articles. Read those that interest you, and delete when done.

Your time is limited. Make every moment count!

Reading

Rate Importance	minus	My Skill Level	equals	Gap
1 2 3 4 5 6 7 8 9 10	–	1 2 3 4 5 6 7 8 9 10	=	_____

Things I'm doing right: _____

_____

_____

_____

What goals can I set to improve in this area? _____

_____

_____

_____

Specific steps that I must take to achieve my improvement goals: _____

_____

_____

_____

_____

Action plan: _____

_____

_____

_____

_____

_____

When I want to complete this: _____

_____

Schools of Management Thought

Not all managers are well-rounded. Your education and training, along with many other influencing factors, impact you as a manager and your views of those you manage. Over time, the field of business management has evolved into various schools of management thought. The following is a listing of some of them:

- The Old School of Hard Knocks
- The Behavior Science School
- The Decision Theory School
- The Empirical School
- The Industrial Dynamics School
- The Management Process School
- The Mathematical School
- The Social System School

The above listing of management theory schools gives you some indication of the options available to you in executing management tasks.

When it becomes necessary for humans to do something, they tend to do what they know how to do. You bring to the task of business management what you've learned in the past, not only what you learned in school, but also from your real-world experiences and observed successes and costly failures.

What you know has an influence on how you approach a task or attempt to solve a specific problem. It also is a determining factor on the types of tasks and problems you avoid. The more tools you have, and know how to use and have experience using, the more likely you are to select a uniquely specific tool that works best for you in the tasks you face now and in the future.

Management has many theoretical schools of thought, and each of these schools has valuable insights to offer the business manager. Management is not theoretical knowledge—its practical knowledge! A well-rounded business manager is a thinker (not a doer), yet he or she must continually be thinking about human activity that they must guide so that human goals may be achieved.

Do you know enough about management theory schools? Do you have enough tools in your toolbox for the jobs you must do? Does one size wrench fit all tasks? The ultimate test of viability and validity comes about when theory becomes practice—when the rubber meets the road!

Schools of Management Thought

Rate Importance	minus	My Skill Level	equals	Gap
1 2 3 4 5 6 7 8 9 10	–	1 2 3 4 5 6 7 8 9 10	=	_____

Things I'm doing right: _____

_____

_____

_____

What goals can I set to improve in this area? _____

_____

_____

_____

Specific steps that I must take to achieve my improvement goals: _____

_____

_____

_____

_____

Action plan: _____

_____

_____

_____

_____

_____

When I want to complete this: _____

_____

Self-Confidence

An important factor in effective management is gaining a high level of self-confidence. You must come to the realization that you not only can (but also will) tackle the tasks at hand and have reasonable expectations of achieving success. There are three things you must develop to gain the level of self-confidence you need: **competence, commitment, and control.**

- **Competence** is built by doing your homework. You can't slow down and expect to succeed if you haven't studied for the test. The only way to have confidence is to know that you've done your best to prepare. Build competence by starting from a success base. Mentally rehearse success. See, feel, and hear the desired end result. Put pressure on the nervous system to create the performance outcome you desire.
- **Work hard.** This simple premise is no guarantee for success, but it's the only way performance will be maximized. With hard work, there's always a chance to succeed. Without it, failure is guaranteed. Self-confidence demands a sincere **commitment** to the task.
- Recognize that there are certain necessary feelings that accompany the state of readiness to perform. Increased heart rate, dry mouth, hollow feeling in the pit of the stomach, and muscle tightness are normal feelings providing notice that the body and mind are ready to meet the challenge. These responses are not indicators of impending failure if they are **controlled.** Nothing can be accomplished without some amount of tension.

Work on taking control over your emotions, thoughts, and goals. Understand that there are factors that are beyond your control. Time should not be wasted worrying about these factors. Concentrate only on the factors over which you can exercise some degree of influence. Don't stare at the approaching train, look where you're putting your feet!

As a manager, you have the opportunity to help others gain greater self-confidence. Keep track of the positive accomplishments of your employees and remind them of their growth. The purpose of these reminders is to continually orient employees as to how far they've grown and developed, and what they can reasonably expect of themselves in the future. Help them visualize what they're capable of. Remind them of what it feels like to perform well, and explain realistically where they stand in terms of what they're capable of today. This kind of attention will foster the self-confidence necessary for individuals to demonstrate again and again what they're capable of. Be careful not to raise expectations to a level they cannot possibly achieve. Reflect for a moment on the following points:

- Personal excellence is largely a matter of believing in one's capabilities and performing with a sense of pride, perseverance and commitment to identified objectives.

Related Topics:
- Confidence and Positive Attitude
- Leadership
- Peer Pressure

- Self-esteem is the strength of one's convictions that they can successfully execute a behavior required to produce a certain outcome.
- Expectations and potential rewards determine how much effort individuals expend and how long they will persist in the face of adversity.

Actual performance is directly related to the individual's feeling of competence and expectations of personal effectiveness.

Self-Confidence

Rate Importance	minus	My Skill Level	equals	Gap
1 2 3 4 5 6 7 8 9 10	–	1 2 3 4 5 6 7 8 9 10	=	_____

Things I'm doing right: _____

_____

_____

_____

What goals can I set to improve in this area? _____

_____

_____

_____

Specific steps that I must take to achieve my improvement goals: _____

_____

_____

_____

_____

Action plan: _____

_____

_____

_____

_____

_____

When I want to complete this: _____

_____

Stress

A simple definition of stress is the way you react physically and emotionally to change. Like change, stress can be either positive or negative. Stress may be the sense of concentration you feel when faced with a new and challenging situation, or it may be the vague sense of anxiety you feel after "one of those days!" In any case, you can learn to manage stress so that you can be in control.

Stress is caused by a sense of frustration—trying to do too many things yourself. It occurs when you run out of time and must carry things over. This is followed by knowing that the "to do's" that get carried over to the next day will be added to a whole new list of "things to do." You then feel boxed in with no escape and no alternatives. To minimize stress—handle what you can, and delegate what you cannot!

Positive Stress
In its positive aspect, stress can help you to concentrate, focus, perform, and can often help you to reach peak efficiency. Many people, in fact, do their best work when under pressure. Then, when the challenge has been met, they take the time to relax and enjoy their achievements. This relaxation response allows them to build up the physical and emotional reserves to meet the next challenge, and is one of the key elements of positive stress.

Negative Stress
Stress becomes negative when you stay "geared-up" and don't (or can't) relax after meeting the challenge. In today's world, where many situations can "push our buttons," it's no wonder. For some people, stress becomes a way of life. Unfortunately, when stress becomes a constant, ongoing cycle, your health and well-being can suffer. Negative stress has been linked with many physical ailments—from tension headaches to heart attacks. The good news is that with proper management, stress need not be hazardous to your health. Don't forget that your stress level impacts not only you, but also those who are around you and love and care for you.

Managing Stress—Awareness
In order to manage stress, it's helpful to know what causes your stress and how you feel when under stress. Try to identify the situations in your life that make you feel tense. Then, "listen" to your body for signs such as headaches, stomach upsets, tensed muscles, clenched teeth, cold or clammy hands, or other symptoms that are indicators that you're under stress.

Relaxation Techniques
As you know, stress can be positive when it is balanced with relaxation. However, when stress is constant and unrelieved, it can become negative and even a destructive force. You can break the cycle of negative stress by learning ways to help yourself relax. By taking the time to

practice simple relaxation techniques on a regular basis, you can give yourself a chance to unwind and get ready for life's next challenge.

Positive Attitude and Lifestyle

A positive attitude and lifestyle are key elements of stress management. Since stress is both an emotional and physical reaction to change, the better you feel (in body and mind), the better you'll be able to deal with the everyday stress in your life. When you learn to think positively, exercise, eat well, and rest regularly, you'll be taking care of the most important person you know—you!

Your stress response is automatic, like blinking your eyes. When faced with a challenging situation, your muscles tense, your heart rate and blood pressure increase, you may perspire more, and you may even notice a gripping sensation in your stomach. You may also feel more mentally alert and focused. This stress response prepares your body to meet an immediate, recognizable challenge.

When stress is **positive,** your body automatically relaxes after you've handled the situation that caused your stress response. Your muscles relax and your heart rate, blood pressure, and other physical functions all return to their normal, pre-stressed state. This relaxation response is the most important aspect of positive stress because it allows you to rest and gather the physical and emotional energy you need to meet the next challenge. Positive stress is a series of heightened alert and relaxation responses that help you deal with the changes and challenges of daily life.

With **negative** stress, there's no true relaxation between one stress "crisis" and the next. When your body remains geared up, physical and emotional strain can result. Left uncontrolled, negative stress can lead to high blood pressure, ulcers, migraines, heart attacks—and worse. Fortunately, you can stop the cycle of negative stress by becoming aware of your stress and how you react to it, by practicing relaxation techniques, and by developing a positive attitude and lifestyle.

Developing a Positive Attitude:

- **Self-talk** means telling yourself what you can or cannot do. Positive self-talk is saying "I can," and setting your mind to meet the challenge at hand.
- **Rehearsal** is a way to prepare for a potentially stressful situation before it occurs. Think over the situation, go over the details, plan to take action, and visualize yourself proceeding successfully.
- **Developing an action plan** can help you turn a stress disaster into a new opportunity. Always make an alternate plan, just in case the one you rehearsed doesn't pan out.

Developing a Positive Lifestyle:

- **Exercise.** Physically fit people handle stress more easily than those who are not since they're apt to feel better about themselves in general. A regular exercise program should include some form of aerobic activity. Aerobic exercise helps your body to use oxygen more efficiently and strengthens your heart and lungs. Running, walking, swimming, and bicycling are all excellent aerobic activities. Stretching exercises are also helpful in relieving tense muscles and improving overall flexibility.

▪ **Nutrition.** When planning your meals, remember that the old saying is true: "you are what you eat!" Junk foods and refined sugars are low in nutritional value and generally high in calories. Food is your body's fuel—so give it "high test!" Plan your meals around servings from the four basic food groups: proteins, dairy products, grains, and fresh fruits and vegetables. Eating well, and limiting your use of salt, sugar, caffeine, and alcohol can promote health and help reduce stress.

▪ **Rest and Relaxation.** You already realize that relaxation is a key to balancing stress, but in addition to specific techniques, try to "slow down" and enjoy your leisure time. Realize that sometimes the best thing you can do for yourself is nothing at all. Don't cram your days off with endless chores—make an effort to relax and enjoy your free time. And, try to get to bed at a reasonable hour, especially if you're under stress. Your body needs sleep to refresh itself, and you need sleep to feel refreshed.

Proper planning and goal setting gives you a sense of stability during the workday. Delegation alleviates some of the responsibility you're carrying. Train employees not to bring problems—bring solutions! And, take time out for personal pursuits with the family, at meetings, hobbies, etc.

Stress

Rate Importance 1 2 3 4 5 6 7 8 9 10	minus –	My Skill Level 1 2 3 4 5 6 7 8 9 10	equals =	Gap _____

Things I'm doing right: _____

_____

_____

_____

What goals can I set to improve in this area? _____

_____

_____

_____

Specific steps that I must take to achieve my improvement goals: _____

_____

_____

_____

_____

Action plan: _____

_____

_____

_____

_____

_____

When I want to complete this: _____

_____

Success and/or Mortality Rate

There is a basic truth to achieving success in business. You must know how to handle people, how to handle problems, and you must know how to handle yourself.

To achieve even a minor level of success, you must establish goals. Decide what has to be done, and then do it. Ideas are important and they're necessary, but they are only the beginning. Ideas must be carried out to have meaning. Something that remains in your mind does no one any good. *If you fail to plan, you plan to fail.* This is one of the reasons why it's so important for managers to manage their own time. You must attend to the day-to-day functions of your business; however, you must also set aside time to think and make plans. That's your job, and if you don't do it—no one else will!

Cooperation and genuine support from others is necessary for attainment of your goals. Failures motivate you to do things you should have done before. So why fail? Do them now!

If you're not getting enough work, not making anticipated profits, or not getting the kind of work you want, reevaluate and concentrate on such potential problems as:

- Bidding the wrong work
- Too many mathematical errors
- Miscalculating overhead—you need more volume
- Poor management and planning
- Problems with staff/employees
- Labor, which is not sufficiently productive
- Lack of a consistent bidding procedure

Under-capitalization is a prime cause of failure. It also prevents expansion. Use your available funds wisely. Put nonworking funds into interest-bearing investments.

Try to get into noncyclical work, and eliminate seasonal variations in volume. Locate your shop as closely as possible to the area where the majority of your work is concentrated, close to your main suppliers, and within easy access to main travel arteries.

When sufficient capital is available, expand your services. Diversify. Keep abreast of the state of the art of your specific industry. Opportunities may present themselves in the future to enter additional markets, which will greatly enhance your firm's financial position.

Consider learning more about taking the right road to success by reading ***The Handbook to Higher Consciousness*** by Ken Keyes, Jr. This book was published in 1989 by Love Line Books and is available online and at some bookstores.

Related Topics:
- Goal Setting
- Time Management

Mike Holt's Business Management Skills Workbook

Success and/or Mortality Rate

Rate Importance 1 2 3 4 5 6 7 8 9 10	minus –	My Skill Level 1 2 3 4 5 6 7 8 9 10	equals =	Gap _____

Things I'm doing right: _____

_____

_____

_____

What goals can I set to improve in this area? _____

_____

_____

_____

Specific steps that I must take to achieve my improvement goals: ___

_____

_____

_____

_____

Action plan: _____

_____

_____

_____

_____

When I want to complete this: _____

_____

Teamwork

The operation of a business is a team task. Let your employees know that they are part of a team. Assure them that each individual's efforts contribute to the team's success and financial well-being of your business.

There is a certain amount of interdependence required of all members of your organization. Although each individual is required to perform to his/her best ability, it's the total performance that determines success or failure.

In order to improve the spirit of teamwork in your organization, underscore how each individual must depend upon the work of others for overall success. Don't overlook your employees as a source of information to improve teamwork. Your employees see you in all situations and are the object of your efforts. Be open to feedback and have the flexibility to change if there's a better alternative.

Teams either pull together or pull apart. When a team pulls apart, conflict and dissension can undermine self-confidence, disrupt concentration and interfere with individual performance. You need key players who will look after your interests. The following will help you get your team to pull together:

Related Topics:
- Motivation
- Delegation

- Help your employees see the consequences of pulling apart—poor individual and team performances, unhappiness, conflict, etc. Then tell them how pulling together will help the team be more successful.
- Hold each individual responsible for promoting this pulling together attitude by supporting and encouraging co-workers.
- Set goals and encourage all employees to work toward achieving these goals.

Empower others through teamwork. Don't be afraid of delegating responsibility to others. If you've followed proper hiring methods, you should have confidence in the individuals you choose to delegate responsibility to.

Teamwork

Rate Importance	minus	My Skill Level	equals	Gap
1 2 3 4 5 6 7 8 9 10	–	1 2 3 4 5 6 7 8 9 10	=	_____

Things I'm doing right: _____

_____

_____

_____

What goals can I set to improve in this area? _____

_____

_____

_____

Specific steps that I must take to achieve my improvement goals: ___

_____

_____

_____

_____

Action plan: _____

_____

_____

_____

_____

_____

When I want to complete this: _____

_____

Theories—Your Attitude Toward Your Employees

A method of classifying manager's attitudes toward their employees has been developed, and it consists of two theoretical groups. As you read through the following, make notes of statements that you agree with and those that you disagree with. This topic will help you to begin to determine what you think and believe about your employees. Be as honest with yourself as you can, which is not as easy as it may at first sound.

Theory X:

- Most people dislike work and will avoid it when they can.
- People must be pushed and threatened with punishment in order to get them to produce enough to achieve company objectives.
- The average worker has very little ambition, wants to be directed, and will avoid responsibility whenever possible.
- Life is not fair; rewards do not follow results.
- Managers must do all of the planning for workers.

Theory Y:

- People naturally want to work, as children want to play.
- People will control themselves in order to achieve goals they set for themselves.
- People's level of commitment to goals and objectives is related to the rewards for the achievement of them.
- Under the proper conditions, people will learn to accept and seek out responsibilities.
- The ability to imagine, demonstrate ingenuity, be creative, and to develop solutions to problems is naturally shared by most people to some degree.
- Most people today work at a level less than what they're capable of achieving, if properly motivated to excel.
- People want to participate in planning their own future.
- They want to contribute to the highest degree that they can.
- They believe that rewards follow results, that the game is fair.
- Managers should only review plans that have been developed in collaboration with the worker, not develop the plan totally for the worker.

In matters of principal—stand like a rock! In matters of style—swim like a fish! Do you have a single management style that works best for you?

Related Topics:
- Delegation
- Motivation
- Schools of Management Thought
- Teamwork

Theories—Your Attitude Toward Your Employees

Rate Importance	minus	My Skill Level	equals	Gap
1 2 3 4 5 6 7 8 9 10	–	1 2 3 4 5 6 7 8 9 10	=	_____

Things I'm doing right: _____

_____

_____

What goals can I set to improve in this area? _____

_____

_____

Specific steps that I must take to achieve my improvement goals: _____

_____

_____

_____

Action plan: _____

_____

_____

_____

_____

When I want to complete this: _____

_____

The Pareto Principle or the 80:20 Rule

The Pareto Principle is based on the work of Italian economist and avid gardener Vilfredo Pareto in 1906. While gardening, Pareto noticed that 80% of the yield of his pea crop came from 20% of the pea pods. He then went on to notice that this same ratio appeared in the distribution of land in Italy, where 80% of the land was owned by 20% of the population.

This laid the ground work for what today is known as the Pareto Principle. In 1937, Dr. Juran, Quality Management pioneer, applied Pareto's observations about economics to a broader body of work. As a result, Dr Juran's observation of the "vital few and trivial many," the principle that 80 percent of the effects come from 20 percent of the causes, became known as Pareto's Principle or the 80/20 Rule.

The impact of this rule can have large consequences for businesses and help them identify where to focus their energy and their money. We can apply this rule to our own business by asking the following questions:

- What 20% of your employees are producing 80% of the productivity of your business?
- Do 20% of your products account for 80% of product sales?
- Do 80% of job delays arise from 20% of the possible causes of delay?
- Do 80% of customer complaints arise from 20% of your customers?

In fact, we can take it further:

Meetings: 80% of the decisions come from 20% of the meeting time
Time Management: 80% of your measurable results and progress will come from just 20% of the items on your daily To-Do list
Interruptions: 80% of a manager's interruptions come from the same 20% of people
Product Defects: 80% of defects typically come from 20% of input errors
Website: 80% of your visitors will see only 20% of your web site pages
Advertising: 20% of your advertising will produce 80% of your campaign's results
Cleaning: 20% time and effort will get 80% clean!

When we look at it this way, it seems obvious to us that most of the effects (80%) come from the smallest number (20%) of causes.

And the lesson for us in our business is to stop wasting precious time and resources on products and services that drain money, energy and time.

- Have a product range? Put your efforts into the 20% that result in 80% of your sales
- Have a sales force? Focus 80% of their energy on the 20% of big purchasers and repeat buyers

- Want to reduce your costs? Identify which 20% are using 80% of the resources—consider charging for those resources, or shift services away
- Have talented people on your staff? Focus their energy in the areas that bring in 80% of your revenue, and be sure they are praised and rewarded for doing so
- Doing marketing? Identify the top 20% of your market and assign it 80% of your efforts
- Having problems getting through your To-Do list? If something's not going to get done make sure it's not part of that 20%

Use of the Pareto Principle or "Pareto Thinking" should become a way of life for you. Your ability to separate the essential from the nonessential will improve with practice, especially if that practice involves use of the actual data and not just "eye-balling" the situation. Once established, this approach becomes a normal reaction to solving problems. In time an experienced "Pareto thinker" can even make quick, accurate judgment calls without taking the time to get the data.

To maximize your personal productivity, realize that of the many things you do during your day, only 20 percent really matter! Identify and focus on those things. What do you do with those that are left over? Either delegate them or discontinue doing them.

Work Smart—identify your 20% now!

The Pareto Principle or the 80:20 Rule

Rate Importance	minus	My Skill Level	equals	Gap
1 2 3 4 5 6 7 8 9 10	–	1 2 3 4 5 6 7 8 9 10	=	_____

Things I'm doing right: _____

_____

_____

_____

What goals can I set to improve in this area? _____

_____

_____

_____

Specific steps that I must take to achieve my improvement goals: _____

_____

_____

_____

_____

Action plan: _____

_____

_____

_____

_____

_____

When I want to complete this: _____

_____

Thinking/Thinking Out Loud

Much of the work of management is done between the ears. Economic conditions must be considered, markets must be investigated, and strategies established. Finances must be set in order. Employee conflicts and frictions must be resolved. To be successful, all of these actions must be preceded by ordered thought.

In all cases, alternatives must be evaluated and a decision must be made. Then, a plan of action must be developed and put in place. Don't close your mind to a single point of view. Listen to others, and determine the proper course of action. Emotions, moods and snap judgments are apt to influence you, but final decisions must be based on clear, careful review of the situation and correct evaluation of the conditions, tempered by special circumstances, timing and priorities. Yes, it is a complex and difficult undertaking!

Many times it will be necessary and advantageous for you to "think on your feet"; that is, make a decision in an instant that could impact your company, other individuals, etc. Developing self-confidence in your ability to think a problem through comes from experience and preparation. Confidence is built using many small parts, such as reading, continuing education, and taking control over your emotions. The foundation of confidence is past success and knowing your own limits. It's difficult to kill a business by trying to make good decisions.

Thinking Out Loud. People hearing you think out loud won't know whether you're expressing an alternative, a random thought, or making a final decision. As a result, they may take action on something you said without realizing it, and it may be a thought you later discarded. Be careful when indulging in this kind of thought process to let any nearby listeners know the status of the statements you make. Remember—he who is in control of his tongue possesses great wisdom!

Thinking/Thinking Out Loud

Rate Importance	minus	My Skill Level	equals	Gap
1 2 3 4 5 6 7 8 9 10	–	1 2 3 4 5 6 7 8 9 10	=	_____

Things I'm doing right: _____

_____

_____

_____

What goals can I set to improve in this area? _____

_____

_____

_____

Specific steps that I must take to achieve my improvement goals: _____

_____

_____

_____

_____

Action plan: _____

_____

_____

_____

_____

_____

When I want to complete this: _____

_____

Time Management

Ask any group of people what they wish they had more of. Some people will say money, of course. Some will say clothes. You'll get various other answers also but the number one answer that crops up the most often is—**TIME.** Time can be wasted, spent foolishly, or invested wisely, but never stored up for future use.

The point is, we don't know how much actual time we have, and since time is such a precious commodity, no one can afford to waste it. Very few of us have memories that can recall our complete daily schedule for priorities, meetings, telephone calls, sales calls, special events, etc., plus what went unfinished the day before. Organize your time and plan your schedule. Don't wait for issues to crop up before you take action—consider your alternatives, and set your plans into operation in time to forestall problems.

Leave time for attention to family, social affairs, personal needs and hobbies. You must determine the importance of specific items as they relate to your business, your personal life, your overall sense of accomplishment, and your needs and self-satisfaction.

Use timesaving technology: Set up organized systems for keeping track of names, addresses, phone numbers, and files. Keep track of your appointments, meetings, and recreational activities on a calendar or smart-phone. Any cost is worthwhile compared to the amount of time and aggravation you can save by eliminating schedule conflicts, missed appointments, etc.

Build a time cushion into your plans: You've made an appointment for Tuesday at 11 a.m. that's scheduled to last for about one hour. You mark it on your calendar and know that you have to set aside one hour for the appointment—**WRONG!** You have other considerations to make—preparing for the appointment, obtaining, reviewing and organizing the materials you'll need, the drive time to and from, if applicable, and returning and putting your materials away. Add this time into your appointment and then add in a little extra time to take into account the unforeseeable delays in getting the job done.

Make quick decisions on small matters: Decisions take energy. Some decisions take a great deal of time, depending on their urgency and complexity. Be reasonable when using this technique. Consider the ramifications of your decision. When you're pushed for time is an excellent opportunity to delegate to others.

Establish systems for handling correspondence: Set up an efficient routine for processing your mail. To shorten time spent on correspondence, use response checklists on which people can quickly indicate a response. Write your own responses to inquiries on the bottom of the original request and return it to the sender. Use standardized forms and form letters, and keep all correspondence materials together in a convenient location. Create a system for filing emails. Handle each piece of paper only once. Use templates, form letters, fax covers, meeting agendas, and other such timesavers. Don't waste time reinventing the wheel; customize and tailor to your needs what is readily available. Chances are several of them are already in your computer that with a little work will not only save you time, but make you appear more professional.

Control your phone time: Keep names and phone numbers current and at arms reach so you won't have to spend time looking for the numbers you want to call. Keep phone conversations to a reasonable length by having a set time of day for making and returning calls. Use an answering machine or service to protect yourself from untimely interruptions if you don't have a secretary or receptionist.

Limit time on the phone by telling callers you only have a few minutes. Rather than discussing points in detail over the phone, ask for or send written materials (by mail or email) which can be reviewed later. Arrange to call back after you or your caller has had time to think over ideas brought up. Practice using a three-minute egg timer to limit the amount of time you talk on the phone. Plan what you're going to say before you place the call. Learn not to waste not only your own time, but others as well. Be always courteous for sure, but efficient as well.

Manage your projects: To manage large projects efficiently, break them down into smaller tasks and list them in the order they need to be completed. Assign deadlines to each task and set up a project file that will serve as the clearinghouse for the entire project. Today there are many good project management systems available. Get one for the entire office. If it's good for you, it will be better for everyone else. On the inside cover of the project file, write the following information in pencil:

- Names, phone numbers and addresses of all people involved
- Tasks to be completed
- Deadlines for each week
- Dates and locations for project meetings

Keep all correspondence and material related to the project in this file. As work progresses, check off the tasks you completed and note any modifications to your project schedule. Consider pre-printing invoices and envelopes when billable projects are first established; billing dates can be handwritten when mailed.

The biggest time-waster is not being able to find information that you need **when you need it.** Use a special technique to prioritize the things you must attend to. For instance, keep things on your desk that are of the highest importance. Put the next most important items in your desk. Pending matters can be placed in the file. Trash anything that's not necessary.

If YOU don't manage YOUR time, someone else will! To-do lists are important in spite of everyone saying they keep getting interrupted and don't finish them. The important point is that if you do get interrupted, you know what didn't get done, and where you left off.

Keep a log of your daily activities to determine how you're spending your time. Keep it faithfully for a period of three days at a minimum. Log everything you do and keep in mind that you want to avoid wasted motion and time.

If you have something to do and can't get it done, plan to complete it the next day or at the next available opportunity. Never allow one missed appointment to cause a delay for the remainder of the day (like the domino effect). Apologize, reschedule, and continue through the day. Get things done, don't waste time!

Take advantage of the various types of time management forms and systems or applications in order to help you manage your time effectively. Employ multitasking when dealing with somewhat routine tasks that do not require your undivided attention. Be sure to allocate sufficient time for pursuit of personal interests.

One last word of advice—**protect your free time!** Everyone needs to take time for relaxation and having fun. Engage in hobbies or other pursuits that you enjoy. Don't become a workaholic.

Related Topics:
- A Balanced Life
- Planning & Organizing

Time Management

Rate Importance	minus	My Skill Level	equals	Gap
1 2 3 4 5 6 7 8 9 10	–	1 2 3 4 5 6 7 8 9 10	=	_____

Things I'm doing right: _____

_____

_____

What goals can I set to improve in this area? _____

_____

_____

Specific steps that I must take to achieve my improvement goals: _____

_____

_____

_____

Action plan: _____

_____

_____

_____

_____

When I want to complete this: _____

_____

Training

Any observer of the labor market will recognize the need to continue training beyond initial trade or professional qualifications. It is essential to maintain, upgrade and update skills—even learn new ones, as we compete for fewer jobs in a changing market.

At least once a year, take a course in some facet of business management. Compare what you've done with what your goals should have been. Ask yourself—What technical skills and certifications have you acquired lately? If you don't have the latest skills and let your customers and potential customers know, you're giving business to the competition.

Knowledge is power, and comes with education and training. The purpose of education is the development of knowledge, which matures into wisdom. Your ability to apply your knowledge influences your earning power. An electrician (for example) who has never taken training classes cannot contribute very much to an organization, nor can they capitalize on opportunities. Encourage your employees, and make it possible for them to train and learn their trade or enhance their skills so that they can first increase their productivity, and then qualify for advancement. One must occur before the other can occur.

Just as employees can learn from you, so can you sometimes learn from them. Very often they come up with a practical solution to a problem, or find a better way to do a specific task. When they do so, publicly acknowledge their unique contribution. You will be pleasantly amazed at how many copycats there are in your firm.

Repetition makes things come easier. Training builds confidence and the task becomes second nature. It's a common misconception that practice makes perfect—it does not! Practice only promotes familiarity. To improve through practice, you must study and analyze your performance during practice, and then improve upon your past performance.

What occurs during training is important to be sure, but what occurs after training is much more important. Training attempts to change something. Supervisors must know what was covered during a training program and follow up to ensure that the training is being applied; that is, that the desired change has occurred. If not, the training activity failed or the trainee failed the true training test.

Today, many trades require continuing education credits. Today's society is changing very rapidly with new areas of opportunity opening almost daily. The better-educated individual is the one who will stand the best chance of achieving success in his or her career.

Develop a formal training plan and fund the budget to accomplish the plan. Include yourself in the plan. Don't try to do all the training in one short period of time—spread it out! This helps to keep the importance of training fresh in everyone's mind.

Training

Rate Importance	minus	My Skill Level	equals	Gap
1 2 3 4 5 6 7 8 9 10	–	1 2 3 4 5 6 7 8 9 10	=	_____

Things I'm doing right: _____

_____

_____

What goals can I set to improve in this area? _____

_____

_____

Specific steps that I must take to achieve my improvement goals: _____

_____

_____

_____

Action plan: _____

_____

_____

_____

When I want to complete this: _____

_____

Weaknesses

Everyone has weaknesses. It's extremely important that you objectively analyze your own individual weaknesses and determine how you can overcome them. Some of the more common weaknesses stated by managers include the following. Alternative actions or corrective measures are also listed.

Weakness: Spelling and Grammar.
Solution: Spell-checkers on computers, or writing tasks assigned to someone with better spelling and grammar skills.

Weakness: Immaturity.
Solution: Consciously developing a sense of maturity, improving problem-solving skills and decision-making, and increasing self-confidence.

Weakness: Temperamental.
Solution: Everyone has feelings, but make a concerted effort not to allow personal problems or feelings to affect decisions and performance on the job. Learn to develop patience. You have a responsibility to others to control your emotions.

Weakness: Can't handle criticism.
Solution: Criticism given improperly often simulates personal attack and results in hard feelings and diminished self-confidence. Know the person who is providing the criticism. If you know the individual is concerned about you and your organization, try to accept constructive criticism graciously. Be open to self-improvement.

Weakness: Perfectionist.
Solution: A real stress-inducer. Perfection is an elusive quality. If you cannot easily change, try not to inflict this trait on others. Be fair and realistic in your dealings with others.

There are obviously many more areas that can be considered weaknesses in an individual. Rather than a rating for this area, take some time to make an objective list of those areas you feel you are weak in. Attempt to come up with alternatives or solutions to overcome these weaknesses. Be careful when you ask others for their appraisal of your weaknesses—you may receive more honesty than anticipated. Be prepared to handle it!

Related Topics:
- Change
- Goal Setting
- Listening and Learning

Weaknesses

Rate Importance	minus	My Skill Level	equals	Gap
1 2 3 4 5 6 7 8 9 10	–	1 2 3 4 5 6 7 8 9 10	=	_____

Things I'm doing right: _____

_____

_____

_____

What goals can I set to improve in this area? _____

_____

_____

_____

Specific steps that I must take to achieve my improvement goals: _____

_____

_____

_____

_____

Action plan: _____

_____

_____

_____

_____

_____

When I want to complete this: _____

_____

Websites and Internet Marketing

The Internet provides a means of marketing your business or services, and its marvels are available to just about everyone who has any type of computer, smart phone or tablet. Your business cannot survive today without being a part of this powerful sales and marketing tool.

With almost one billion Web pages available for some of us, the Internet may look more like a bowl of spaghetti than an information super-highway. A Web page can be likened to a small store in a strip mall off of the freeway in that it provides a location for marketing your business and its services, but it must be readily accessible to be of any value to your customers.

Create your Webpage

Your Website is your face, your brand and your key marketing tool. It must provide content that visitors (hopefully your potential customers) will find appealing and be of value. This content and the way you arrange it are influenced by what you hope your pages will accomplish. Your Website can take this information content and make it "interactive" where customers can click, learn, and understand why you are an expert, and perhaps their best contracting choice.

- If you're not confident about your design skills, it's best to keep it very simple or hire professionals to do this work.
- Develop content that will appeal to your customers, which will help you in achieving your marketing and sales goals. Scout the Internet looking for tips, graphic ideas and layouts that may be appealing to you. Use this freedom to experiment with ideas and learn from the feedback of visitors. One of the advantages of building a Website is that nothing is physical or permanent. If you don't like the looks of something you've done, it can be revised quickly. Just remember that everything you do has a cost to acquire and a cost to maintain.
- Usability and the utility, more than the visual design, will determine the success or failure of your site. It should:
  - Be obvious and self-explanatory
  - Easy to navigate
  - Focus on what's important
  - Simple and easy to scan
  - Use images wherever possible
- Use the search feature on the internet for "effective websites" and select the elements of design and functionality that are highly rated and appealing to you, and adapt elements for your own use.
- Request feedback. As the name information super-highway implies, Web pages are about information—the giving and receiving of information. Be sure to get what information you can from your visitors. What were they looking for? What did they like? Include easy ways for those who browse your digital store to give you feedback.

Feedback is the corrective signaling element in an information management system.
Without it, you're bowling blind.

Let your webpage advertise for you:

Your Website offers a compelling message to an eager audience and it has advantages others can't touch. Use it to find new prospects and customers. In the world of computers, names and addresses are important—even magical. Start simple and let the site grow at a pace that suits you.

- Give people a reason to read and return to your Website. New or improved business services could be one of the main reasons. It's important that whatever you decide upon, you must make a clear plan of action with set deadlines and realistic aims.
- Websites have a tendency to be highly impersonal. Write like you speak. Tell prospects why you care about them and earning their business. Insert an electronic signature and/or a photo of the letter writer.
- Develop a way to thank customers for their visit and interest in your business or services. Providing some form of free service has been a traditional means of thanking visitors to your site.
- Do whatever it takes to grab the reader's attention
- Plan where on your site you put your "opt-in" offer—your tool for gathering your customer's email address which allows you to regularly keep in touch with them through newsletters or product/service offerings. Where it appears on your site can have a huge impact on how many subscribers you get [every page, home page, in every letter, etc]. .Get contact information. If you don't do this, it's like NOT putting your phone number in an ad. Get names or you're lost!
- Add impact to your promotions with hover ads. This is a new technology that lets you use ads that behave like pop-ups, that that aren't pop-ups so they don't get blocked.
- Feature the benefits of your services in your headline to grab their attention and compel them to read further. Make it clear to your customer what your service will do for them.
- Testing is the only way to find out what works and what doesn't—you just never know what strategy or angle will work best for you until you try it out.

Maximize your exposure

In order to capitalize on your market you need to understand how your online marketing efforts are performing and how you can improve on them. Understanding metrics can help you identify issues such as inconsistent search phrases, incorrect definitions, etc. The proper use of key words (among other techniques) can help a website go to the top of a search, which is the key make or break factor for many new businesses.

There are countless Search Engine Optimization (SEO) experts and consultants who claim they can get your site in Google's top 10 search results. Before you take on this expensive route, do proper research. It has been said that a huge percentage of the SEO business is scam, and many unscrupulous firms make promises they can't keep or use practices that are not strictly above board. Your best bet is to research and understand how the key words and phrases and other techniques affect your ranking on the search and make sure that you or your web designer or copy writer uses all the proper tools, tricks and techniques at all times. If your website has a great design and functionality, and your reputation is good, you should rise to the top!

Marketing

Your website should be as much a part of your branding as your company name and logo. Include your Web address (your URL) in all of your other media, and your phone, fax and physical address on your Web pages. Just as your shoes, pants and shirt should all match, so too should all of your advertising. Compare the flavor, tone and theme of your Web pages to your other advertisements. They should all flow together like a stream of intelligent media.

It is futile (and perhaps foolish) to invest in a Website without these goals. Your goal is to get prospects, inform them, and then move them to customers as fast as possible. Start today and expand your Internet marketing power by either creating or improving your website and making it compelling and functional. With perseverance, experimentation, grim determination and a sprinkling of luck, you'll find that it's well worth the effort.

Start small and build on your success.

Related Topics:
- Advertising and Branding
- Computers and Technology
- Marketing

Websites and Internet Marketing

Rate Importance	minus	My Skill Level	equals	Gap
1 2 3 4 5 6 7 8 9 10	−	1 2 3 4 5 6 7 8 9 10	=	_____

Things I'm doing right: _____

_____

_____

_____

What goals can I set to improve in this area? _____

_____

_____

_____

Specific steps that I must take to achieve my improvement goals: _____

_____

_____

_____

_____

Action plan: _____

_____

_____

_____

_____

_____

When I want to complete this: _____

_____

Chapter

Financial Management

Knowing how to manage your business can take you only so far if you lose sight of the bottom line. You're in business to make a profit so you can stay in business, and managing your money is the key. Your profitability will depend on the total overview of your organization, including employee management and job management as well as all factors involved in general business management. The purpose of this chapter is to review factors that relate to the finances of your business.

As a business owner/manager, you must constantly monitor the bottom line of your income statement to be sure that expenses are not exceeding income. You should keep in mind that pursuing overall profitability necessitates remaining informed of the current conditions of multiple financial factors in the process of managing the activities of your business. A manager is the template for multi-tasking abilities. You must keep all of the financial balls properly juggled in the air, at the right place, time, and velocity.

You need not go it alone. Professional special team members and consultants are readily available to lend an attentive ear, judge options and develop executable business plans for large, small, new or well-established firms. Professionals focus on stressing financial performance enhancement while developing and enhancing competitive advantages through the exercise of proven management expertise.

Chapter 2—Financial Management
Table of Contents

Accounting

Having a strong accounting system in place is essential for your business to survive and grow. Here are five key things you need to remember when analyzing your business financial documents:

Count your money

Understanding the financial picture of your organization is crucial. You have to count your money! You are not in business for practice, and the fastest way to go out of business is to lose track of your money and your cash flow. You need to know your costs on jobs and how much money you have as you navigate each step of running your business. The way to start is to have a well-prepared financial statement. There are basically four different types:

- A Balance Sheet
- An Income Statement (also called Profit & Loss statement)
- Statement of Retained Earnings
- Statement of Cash Flow

Your Financial Statement should be prepared by a qualified accountant using generally accepted accounting principals (GAAP) since these documents will be the records that you use to make all your business decisions. Another great tool to help you improve your understanding of accounting is to buy a basic accounting book so that you are familiar with the numbers that are the scorecard of your business.

Make a Budget

Your financial budget is a projection of your future and desired goals, and a plan for its attainment expressed in dollar amounts. At the beginning of your company's fiscal (record keeping) year, you should have established a budget based on your objectives. If you didn't do that, you need to do that now. If you don't know what your goals are, you will not be equipped to make the right decisions to get you there. If you don't have the luxury of a full-time employee to prepare your financial statements, the least you need to do is to hire a professional to prepare your annual budget and to teach you what you need to know to complete the monthly bookkeeping. If you are in a position where you are having to create your own budget, then you need to be as educated as you can be, do the research on the Internet, the library or at the bookstore on what it takes to have a successful business budget.

Maintain your books

It is critical that you study your monthly statements (results of operations), and compare them with your budget (plan) to see how close you're coming to your objectives (goals). Studying financial statements will enable you to understand the current financial health of your business, and make necessary adjustments on a timely basis. The statement represents a financial record of what is happening to your business, and enables you to handle problems when they are discovered, instead of waiting until they become unmanageable.

Understand your costs

Overhead refers to the ongoing expenses of operating a business without consideration of any costs allocated or associated with specific jobs. Understanding these costs, especially when business is slow, is the most important factor in managing your finances. Estimating, which is an essential part of the contracting and service trades, is dependent on the accuracy of the overhead shown in your financial statement. If you don't know how much you need to sell to cover your expenses, you won't know how to estimate your jobs. Finding work is hard enough—the last thing you need is to lose money because you don't understand what your true costs are.

Some costs will remain relatively constant from one financial statement to the next—occupancy, taxes, licenses, bonding, fees, utilities, etc. Unless there is a radical change in the size of your business this cost will not vary much from one month to the next. If your business is struggling, moving to smaller facilities can make a big change in your overhead. If your business is very successful and has outgrown your current facility, expansion or moving to larger offices comes hand in hand with increased rent, equipment, office help, etc., and your total overhead will increase. If you add one or two more employees, you'll probably occupy the same facilities and pay the same fees, such as licenses, utilities, etc. The total increase in overhead will vary only slightly and the cost of overhead per field employee will be reduced. Personnel costs are part of your overhead; usually administrative staff would be part of your overhead, and project personnel would be allocated to a job—your accountant should advise you how to handle these costs in your business.

If your company is primarily in the servicing business, the separation of truck overhead from other fixed overhead items might not be significant. In this type of business, for each employee there is a vehicle and the number of vehicles is increased or reduced with the change in the number of service personnel. In construction, there is not a constant relationship in the number of employees per truck; therefore, to create a more accurate financial picture, when you get to estimating, you would allocate your overhead in a more practical manner by maintaining fixed truck overhead as a separate item on your financial statement. Certain jobs may not require the use of trucks on locations where you put a trailer in place. Therefore, the cost of the trailer must be included in your job-cost estimate, but you may eliminate the overhead associated with the cost directly related to the trucks.

When you understand that your estimates have to include your overhead burdens and profit (the cost exposure to the risk of doing business) as well as the cost of direct labor, required materials and other costs relating to the job, you start to understand the importance of your monthly financial statements.

It is also important to keep track of discounts and deals made with customers. Working with friends and families "require" some sort of discount, so keep track of what percentage of profit was lost. When you are adding up your monthly or quarterly Profit/Loss Sheet, you may be unpleasantly surprised what your profits could/should have been.

Owner's Expense/Owner's Bonus

It is just as important to have a personal/family budget and financial statement as it is to have one for your business. The item on the statement headed "Owner's Bonus" or "Owner's Expenses" is a catchall for owner's expenses paid by the business. As an owner, you take the financial risk, so you are entitled to a greater share of the profits. However, when you are struggling to make decisions about your business expenses this would be an area where you have more flexibility. Understanding what you need financially on a personal level is critical—if you are failing financially in your personal life, there is no hope for your business. Talk to your CPA or tax attorney to make sure that you are taking advantage of legally permissible business deductions here and elsewhere to reduce your tax burden.

No matter what stage your business is at, now is the time to study your financial statements. Examine all of your expenses and outflow. By knowing where each penny of your money is going you will be able to identify every item that can be reduced, eliminated or even increased so you can make healthy decisions for your business. Once you have a clear picture of what you have to do, you can make your plan and take control—focus on one project at a time.

Accounting

Rate Importance	minus	My Skill Level	equals	Gap
1 2 3 4 5 6 7 8 9 10	–	1 2 3 4 5 6 7 8 9 10	=	_____

Things I'm doing right: _____

_____

_____

What goals can I set to improve in this area? _____

_____

_____

Specific steps that I must take to achieve my improvement goals: _____

_____

_____

_____

Action plan: _____

_____

_____

_____

_____

When I want to complete this: _____

Bad Debt

An organization's financial loss due to nonpayment of monies due it is referred to as bad debt. Bad debts are a direct result of the credit policy and management of credit terms by your company. The credit policy reflects the desire and ability of your company to assume the financial risk of loss associated with providing customers with the benefits of credit. While credit should be granted only after an evaluation of the credit worthiness of the applicant, no evaluation procedure will ever be totally accurate. Your company will likely have some bad debts.

Unfortunately, this is part of running a business, and the obvious goal is to keep bad debts as low as possible. If your gross profit is 20 percent, you need five times the amount of the bad debt in additional volume to offset the lost profit. By conducting proper credit checks on customers, and by managing collection and billing procedures, you can help keep bad debts down to a minimum. Credit, like other business functions, must be managed in a timely fashion.

Keeping track of the percentage of bad debt losses to sales income is necessary so that you can include this cost in future bids. This will help to improve the accuracy of your estimates of the true cost of doing business when preparing bids.

Related Topics:
- Accounting
- Billing and Collecting
- Collection/ Collection Procedures

Bad Debt

Rate Importance	minus	My Skill Level	equals	Gap
1 2 3 4 5 6 7 8 9 10	–	1 2 3 4 5 6 7 8 9 10	=	_____

Things I'm doing right: _____

_____

_____

_____

What goals can I set to improve in this area? _____

_____

_____

_____

Specific steps that I must take to achieve my improvement goals: _____

_____

_____

_____

_____

Action plan: _____

_____

_____

_____

_____

_____

When I want to complete this: _____

Bankers/Line of Credit

Invest the time necessary to find a good banker and develop a close working relationship, and then stick with them should they move to another lender. If you have a problem locating a banker you can work with, ask your accountant, attorney, stockbroker, or other respected advisors in the financial field to recommend a banker and to arrange an introduction. In order to be successful, you must not allow a small-thinking attitude to inhibit your financial growth, even if it requires securing loans to grow.

On occasion, a requirement for operating funds comes up suddenly, perhaps for new equipment, or to finance a large contract. As most businesses do not have the amount of financial capital necessary for daily operations and to fund needed growth, a source of external credit must be established. Credit can be obtained from either short term (high-rate credit cards) or more formal and less costly long-term arrangements, such as working capital-type lines of credit.

A line of credit is an agreement between your firm (typically you individually) and a financial institution (such as your local bank) that agrees to provide a specific amount of money that will be available when needed during the agreement's term (usually one or more years). Establishing a line of credit is essential since you cannot run a business without adequate funds. The cost and ease of obtaining credit is based on experience and confidence. Even if you don't need extra cash in the early stages, establish a pattern of borrowing money in increasingly larger amounts. Make payments on time to establish the lender's confidence in you.

A line of credit usually requires a personal guarantee. It's no longer easy to find a credit line based solely on a corporate guarantee. Always review with your attorney the potential risk to your personal assets in the event of default on all loans.

When securing a loan, consider borrowing against your receivables if this option is available to you. Given the propensity for mergers among lenders, after you've built up a proven track record, spread your financial business to perhaps two additional sources of capital.

Bankers/Line of Credit

Rate Importance	minus	My Skill Level	equals	Gap
1 2 3 4 5 6 7 8 9 10	–	1 2 3 4 5 6 7 8 9 10	=	_____

Things I'm doing right: _____

_____

_____

What goals can I set to improve in this area? _____

_____

_____

Specific steps that I must take to achieve my improvement goals: _____

_____

_____

_____

Action plan: _____

_____

_____

_____

When I want to complete this: _____

_____

Billing and Collecting

You can't manage a business without money, so you have to know where the money is coming from, and when it is coming. If you do the work, you should get paid. If you don't get paid, don't do the work!

Customers who routinely delay payment as a matter of policy should become ex-customers. Customers who delay payment due to genuine financial causes are potentially placing your firm in the same financial condition that they are in. Be firm, fair and financially sound. Get paid on time!

Billing

Your billings produce your cash flow so each day that you delay billing your customers, you negatively impact your cash flow. You need the funds in your account (not your customer's) not only to enable you to pay your own bills, but to reduce the amount of interest expense associated with borrowed money.

Statistics show that the longer a bill remains unpaid, the less chance you have of collecting. Get your collection procedures established and working properly.

- Your billing must be accurate to eliminate delays in adjusting discrepancies.
- Prompt billing gets the invoice to the customer while the details of the job are fresh in their minds.
- The sooner the invoice is received and approved by the customer, the sooner you're apt to receive payment. Remember, there is no embarrassment in asking for money when it is due.
- Keep accurate records of changes and extras in your installations, and see that the proper charges are included. Be clear to avoid confusion.
- Follow up on delinquent accounts with a letter, email or personal phone-call. Assume the best, perhaps there's a misunderstanding that can be resolved by making contact with the debtor. If you are sending a letter or an email, you might want to set up a template for yourself, to standardize the process. The letter should thank them for their business, and kindly remind them that their payment is late.
- Start collection procedures as soon as the invoice is past due.
- Issue duplicate invoices immediately when the customer claims the original was not received. If you have the customer's email address, email them an invoice, and select the email option to request a "receipt" when the email is opened.
- Make a photocopy of every payment received. These duplicate records help to determine whether a payment was actually made. At some future date, you may want to have information regarding this customer's bank and its address. Retaining copies of their checks will provide a record of this information.

Collecting:

- Determine who is responsible for collections.
- Establish a written procedure.
- Send a friendly reminder immediately when the bill is due.
- Delegate responsibility for collections to someone who is strong-willed and firm.

Never let anything get over 30 days past due. If you let your accounts receivables go past 30 days, it shows a court and the lender you are not a business just a hobby. Hire a bookkeeper that has collection experience. Make sure he or she is nice; because you will get paid with a spoonful of honey, and will get a battle with an ounce of acid.

Mechanic's Lien:

You have various options in collecting unpaid invoices. Perfecting a Mechanic's Lien prior to starting the job is a good investment. Don't allow the customer to insert a clause denying you this right. If the debtor is temporarily short of funds, work out a deferred payment plan over a period of time, charging interest until fully paid. If all else fails, use the courts in a lawsuit, or engage the services of a collection agency. Be prepared for major losses when your in-house collection efforts fail and you pass the task onto others.

Before filing that mechanics lien do everything you can yourself to collect. Small claims court will not be too happy that you did not exhaust all best efforts. Get it in writing what your client disputes, and try to work it out with them. Remember you always look for a win-win, but do not work for free, especially if you did everything right according to plans. Shoot for zero tolerance in your work and all your subs work and hold your subs accountable. You reputation requires it.

To file a preliminary lien notice is not very hard, just make sure you record it at your county's recorder office where the work is being done, not your office location, and send copies to the lender. That way the lender will be on your side to collecting the debt.

Customers who routinely delay payment as a matter of policy should become ex-customers. Customers who delay payment due to genuine financial causes are potentially placing your firm in the same financial condition that they are in. Be firm, fair and financially sound. Get paid on time!

Related Topics:
- Bad Debt
- Legal

Billing and Collecting

Rate Importance	minus	My Skill Level	equals	Gap
1 2 3 4 5 6 7 8 9 10	–	1 2 3 4 5 6 7 8 9 10	=	_____

Things I'm doing right: _____

_____

_____

_____

What goals can I set to improve in this area? _____

_____

_____

_____

Specific steps that I must take to achieve my improvement goals: ___

_____

_____

_____

_____

Action plan: _____

_____

_____

_____

_____

_____

When I want to complete this: _____

_____

Bonding

It's important to check the local and state requirements for bonding and insurance in the area in which you conduct your business. Every growing business faces different challenges and a unique set of risks.

Surety bonds are occasionally required on some construction projects to ensure that any damage done will be repaired (heavy trucks cracking concrete driveways, for example). Surety bonds can be likened to an insurance policy and are very low cost.

Some types of bids routinely require that a type of surety bond (called a bid bond) be accompanied with a bid for it to be considered. These are also insurance policies, the purpose of which is to provide a source of funds should it become necessary to complete the project in the event that the bidder's company goes out of business before completion of the project. The cost of such bid bonds is routinely listed separately on bid documents. On occasion, the project owner or public entity will elect to delete a bond, in favor of a reduction in the project's cost.

Many contractors will never need to obtain and provide such a bond. After a reputation is established, bonding may not be required. To secure a bond, a contractor must show that he or she has three to four years of financial records reviewed by a Certified Public Accountant, show substantial financial assets over liabilities, and meet other minimum requirements such as having successfully completed projects of comparable size and complexity.

Related Topics:
• Insurance

Bonding

Rate Importance	minus	My Skill Level	equals	Gap
1 2 3 4 5 6 7 8 9 10	–	1 2 3 4 5 6 7 8 9 10	=	_____

Things I'm doing right: _____

_____

_____

_____

What goals can I set to improve in this area? _____

_____

_____

_____

Specific steps that I must take to achieve my improvement goals: _____

_____

_____

_____

Action plan: _____

_____

_____

_____

_____

When I want to complete this: _____

_____

Break-Even Point

Related Topics:
• Accounting
• Budgeting

Break-even is the minimum amount of sales needed to cover expenses. That volume of financial activity at which you could continue in business indefinitely without making a profit is called your break-even point; however, the reason you are in business is to make a profit. So, if your profit and loss statement doesn't show a profit, you're not achieving your goal. You're simply receiving back what was expended during the current recorded period.

Breaking even today does not return the losses occurred in the past, or build up a reserve for future losses, or provide a return on your investment (the reward for exposure to risk). With all business activities, there are risks. When an equitable reward is earned, a return is honorable. There's nothing sinful about making a profit. It's just hard to do!

Contractors are not in the business of selling the job at or below cost. Once you determine the estimated break-even cost of the job, you need to determine the selling price.

Establish a policy of posting deposits and bills daily, including payroll. Use these figures to determine your average bill. After a full year of tracking, you'll be able to determine your average daily bill and your average daily deposits. You can then plot these figures because it's based on a year-to-year average. You will then know what you have to do each day.

When your deposits peak, you can learn to anticipate when heavy expenses will come. You'll then be in a better position to anticipate the "lean" times and compensate for them in advance.

Break-Even Point

Rate Importance	minus	My Skill Level	equals	Gap
1 2 3 4 5 6 7 8 9 10	–	1 2 3 4 5 6 7 8 9 10	=	_____

Things I'm doing right: _____

_____

_____

_____

What goals can I set to improve in this area? _____

_____

_____

_____

Specific steps that I must take to achieve my improvement goals: _____

_____

_____

_____

_____

Action plan: _____

_____

_____

_____

_____

_____

When I want to complete this: _____

_____

Budgeting

Establish your firm's financial goals as realistically as you can, taking into account:

- General business conditions
- Competition
- Size of the marketing area
- Financial capitalization
- Number and skills of your employees
- Your own management and leadership skills

Determine your objectives and then prepare a financial budget. This becomes your firm's financial statement for a fixed period of time (usually one year). It's based on estimates of expenditures for each business function, and includes direct costs and overhead, plus an estimate of anticipated sales volume necessary to cover the expenditures and leave the desired net profit.

New businesses will require the use of estimates, which may later prove to be little more than wishful guesses. Established businesses will have a history to draw upon from which accurate projections of income and expenses can be developed. The following questions are well worth the time it will take to correctly answer them:

- How fast do you want to grow?
- Are there any problems to be expected regarding the availability of a suitable labor supply?
- Sources of financial credit?
- Availability of materials?

As you receive your quarterly financial statements from your accountant, use them as a guideline to see how closely your progress is adhering to budget, and to make any necessary changes in planning, policy or objectives. Income statements are results; budgets are scorecards comparing established goals to actual performance. Comparing what you thought you could accomplish with what you actually accomplished can be a very humbling and motivating task.

Your supply of cash influences every aspect of the financial health of your company. Know what your cash balance is at all times. Don't overlook the importance of billing and collection, which will help you maintain an adequate flow of cash. When more cash is available, budgets can be more liberal. Some owners read the record of billings, sales, deposits and checks written every day before they do anything else. These amounts are vital business condition indicators and tell them what areas require their attention each day. Business today must be run by the numbers, not by gut-level feelings. Know your numbers, your business health numbers, cash, accounts receivable, accounts payable, backlog, etc.

Keep excess operating funds working at all times by placing them in savings accounts or other investments where they will earn a return, until you experience a delay in getting full payment due to billing approval delays, retainage, or slow collection. Where projects are to be delayed for long periods, review your contract and begin to develop a change order so that you can get paid for additional costs arising from material inflation.

With proper forecasting and budgeting techniques, you'll be able to figure out what's needed to cover debt service cost. Once the budget is established, decide if you're going to do something, or who's going to do it, how it should get done, and then continue to track income and expenses by percentages. Once you get a job, forecast billings and collections to determine when to anticipate money coming in. It's difficult to predict cash flow, but with planning and plotting you can estimate or learn to anticipate cash-flow trends. The monitoring of your firm's current cash condition is vital to continued operations.

Maintain records of billing and deposits, cost per day, etc. Determine your billing cycles and keep records accordingly. The added effort in maintaining these records will pay off by providing you with accurate figures for future bids and compensation for the lean times. You want to know where you are, where you're going, and when you'll get there. Look to history and keep good records. They're good sources of guidance for producing future projections.

Related Topics:
- Accounting
- Billing & Collecting
- Payment Schedules
- Record Keeping

Budgeting

Rate Importance	minus	My Skill Level	equals	Gap
1 2 3 4 5 6 7 8 9 10	–	1 2 3 4 5 6 7 8 9 10	=	_____

Things I'm doing right: _____

_____

_____

What goals can I set to improve in this area? _____

_____

_____

Specific steps that I must take to achieve my improvement goals: _____

_____

_____

_____

Action plan: _____

_____

_____

_____

_____

When I want to complete this: _____

_____

Contracts

Don't accept a job without a contract. To do so would be to sow the seeds of controversy, misunderstanding, argument, delayed payments, and erosion of the customer/contractor relationship.

Usually the price and other conditions of a job are agreed on by the act of your presenting a contract, and an authorized representative of the customer signing it. Never begin work before a contract has been signed and is in your possession. Review in detail yourself all contracts presented to your company. Large developers and general contractors have their own contracts that are biased in their favor, but that doesn't mean that you have to sign it as is.

If you're required to sign their contract form, consider striking out clauses that you object to. But, before you begin to do so, ask your lawyer to explain things such as contract terms, acceptance and rejections. Then, prepare to negotiate, and defend your strikeouts. You may have to inflate your price to accommodate special requirements that they insist on. You can prepare a proposal with your own conditions, and make it an addendum to the customer's contract. Prepare a checklist indicating whether you or the customer is responsible for each service.

Anything in the gray area of doubt, such as who pays for temporary power, who patches holes, whether special bonding or insurance is required, etc., should be discussed and agreed on. Be sure that you investigate and know the requirements for licensing, insurance and permitting, as well as the local building codes. Not knowing can be expensive, and not complying can be more expensive.

Contracts, both verbal and written are legal in nature. Know what you're signing and agreeing to!

Related Topics:
- Legal
- Proposals

Contracts

Rate Importance	minus	My Skill Level	equals	Gap
1 2 3 4 5 6 7 8 9 10	–	1 2 3 4 5 6 7 8 9 10	=	_____

Things I'm doing right: _____

_____

_____

_____

What goals can I set to improve in this area? _____

_____

_____

_____

Specific steps that I must take to achieve my improvement goals: _____

_____

_____

_____

_____

Action plan: _____

_____

_____

_____

_____

_____

When I want to complete this: _____

_____

Debt Free

Advantages of being Debt Free:

- When you are free from debt, you enjoy a great deal of freedom and flexibility that you can not experience when you have heavy financial commitments.
- A business that is free from debt has a level of stability and security that makes it possible to work at a higher level of profitability.
- Not being governed by heavy payment deadlines increases your ability to be more able to choose your work to fit your team's talents and experience and maximize your profitability.

If you are not free from debt, consider making that a high priority.

Debt Free

Rate Importance	minus	My Skill Level	equals	Gap
1 2 3 4 5 6 7 8 9 10	−	1 2 3 4 5 6 7 8 9 10	=	_____

Things I'm doing right: _____

_____

_____

_____

What goals can I set to improve in this area? _____

_____

_____

_____

Specific steps that I must take to achieve my improvement goals: _____

_____

_____

_____

_____

Action plan: _____

_____

_____

_____

_____

_____

When I want to complete this: _____

_____

Equipment Rental/ Leasing/Purchase

Advantages of Leasing:

- A lessee (the person to whom property is leased) can enjoy the use of an asset without a large initial cash outlay.
- There's no down payment. A loan may require 25 percent down, where a lease is usually 100 percent financed.
- There are no restrictions on a company's financial operations.
- Payments are spread over a longer period of time.
- You have protection against equipment obsolescence.
- There are tax benefits. Some include deductibility of lease payments as operating expenses if the arrangement is a true lease. Also, the lessor usually takes all of the investment tax credit, but it may help the lessee since the lessee may have reduced payments in return. See your accountant before committing to a lease to verify tax effects.
- You benefit from consulting advice from the leasing firm.
- Payment schedules are flexible.
- There are restrictions on claims in the event of bankruptcy.

Disadvantages of Leasing:

- There's a loss of certain tax benefits. Tax benefits that go with ownership of an asset are not available to a lessee.
- There's no economic value of an asset at the end of the lease term.
- There's higher overall cost in purchase.
- Lease termination is difficult.

The lease represents a senior debt obligation. Although in the event of bankruptcy, claims of a lessor to the assets of a firm are more restricted than those of general creditors, a lease may be one of the first debts that can be claimed by a creditor. When it comes to deciding whether to lease or purchase, some follow the general guideline that "if it appreciates, own it—if it depreciates, lease it."

Equipment Rental/Leasing/Purchase

Rate Importance	minus	My Skill Level	equals	Gap
1 2 3 4 5 6 7 8 9 10	–	1 2 3 4 5 6 7 8 9 10	=	_____

Things I'm doing right: _____

_____

_____

_____

What goals can I set to improve in this area? _____

_____

_____

_____

Specific steps that I must take to achieve my improvement goals: _____

_____

_____

_____

_____

Action plan: _____

_____

_____

_____

_____

When I want to complete this: _____

_____

Expansion, Growth and Stability

Many contractors develop a niche in the market. At times, the local market will be expanding or contracting depending on technology, the economy, and customer needs. Consider every estimate request an opportunity to monitor the market's direction.

When planning for expansion, keep two goals in mind:

The first is that it's logical to expand the kind of work you do best. Contact prospects that are in the same line of business with that of your customers (perhaps its gas stations or convenience food stores). Because of your familiarity with this work, you'll be able to estimate more accurately and increase your chances of getting the job. Your reputation and expertise will precede you. Further efficiencies can result from your setting up a truck with the materials needed for a specific type of job, driven by an employee experienced in this work. On the other hand, if there's certain work that you don't want, bid on something else. Some of the factors to consider are financial gain, profit, economic benefit, equity building, and effective asset utilization when planning for expansion.

The second goal in expansion is to recognize which areas of the industry are growing, and to get there ahead of the competition. Being in the lead not only gives you the opportunity to make higher profits, but it also helps you establish your reputation in this new growth area. Whatever the new technology is, there are manufacturers and distributors of these specialized items that will be glad to provide training on installation and service. Very often this work can be done at the same time you're on the job doing standard electrical installation.

Determine the dollar value of the jobs you can do efficiently. While the dollar range is important, you must consider all factors including labor, material, overhead, profit and taxes. The markup, material/labor mix, and the firm's marketing plan along with the job's specific contribution to overhead give a better picture of the value of a job than just the dollar range. The timing, location and credit worthiness of the owners, along with who the general contractor is, are also items of value that should be considered when the decision to bid a job is made.

Start small and keep employment stable. Grow from a solidly established base. Employees who develop confidence in their job and their company grow to become "company men and women." At that point, you know you can count on your people. You can't get good employees with only short-term intent and with no benefits or stability. Your employees have needs (such as food, clothing, and shelter to name but a few) that they hope and expect to achieve by doing their jobs. We all have needs, and continuous employment in challenging, gratifying work is a major source of obtaining our individual needs.

Expansion, Growth and Stability

Rate Importance	minus	My Skill Level	equals	Gap
1 2 3 4 5 6 7 8 9 10	–	1 2 3 4 5 6 7 8 9 10	=	_____

Things I'm doing right: _____

_____

_____

_____

What goals can I set to improve in this area? _____

_____

_____

_____

Specific steps that I must take to achieve my improvement goals: _____

_____

_____

_____

_____

Action plan: _____

_____

_____

_____

_____

_____

When I want to complete this: _____

_____

Insurance

Every growing business faces different challenges and a unique set of risks. Risks can never be totally eliminated; however, they can be managed through the judicious procurement of insurance policies.

You can obtain insurance for almost any potential adverse event. This part of overhead is necessary to provide some level of protection against losses that could possibly put you out of business. If you're not already, you should become familiar with standard policies, such as bonding, liability, workers' compensation, and health and life insurance as employee benefits.

- Workers' compensation protects your business against liability and, at the same time, ensures that your valued employees have the protection they need if they suffer a serious injury on the job.
- General liability insurance protects business owners and operators from liability exposures that exist broadly across your company, and at multiple locations.
- Professional liability insurance is designed to protect today's professionals against liability incurred as a result of errors and omissions in performing professional services.
- Completed operations insurance covers liability after a job is completed and you've left the jobsite. Theft might include a blanket policy for materials and tools on service trucks, and also your jobsite trailer.
- Key man insurance will pay the estate to buy out the equity of a partner or stockholder in the event of his/her death.

Conduct a detailed review of your firm's insurance policies and undertake a current risk analysis review every five years, or when conditions change so as to warrant it. You need to gauge your firm's liability exposure and put the right solutions in place to bridge the gaps.

Think of other specialized policies you need, such as storefront insurance should you rent a store. There are many risks associated with the operation of a business. While some may say that you can never have too much insurance, you most assuredly can have too little of the correct type. Occasionally, you can manage risk easier than you can produce the additional profit needed to pay for the insurance.

Related Topics:
- Bonding

Insurance

Rate Importance	minus	My Skill Level	equals	Gap
1 2 3 4 5 6 7 8 9 10	–	1 2 3 4 5 6 7 8 9 10	=	_____

Things I'm doing right: _____

_____

_____

_____

What goals can I set to improve in this area? _____

_____

_____

_____

Specific steps that I must take to achieve my improvement goals: _____

_____

_____

_____

_____

Action plan: _____

_____

_____

_____

_____

_____

When I want to complete this: _____

_____

Job Costing
(Estimating Analysis)

In order to project the potential amount of profit or loss that results from each job, you must prepare a job-costing analysis. Not only does job costing act as a measure of the accuracy of your estimating abilities, but of your success and failures of project management as well. Over time, the historical data that it provides gives you a basis for more accurate estimating of similar jobs that you get in the future. When reviewing actual job cost, compare the figures with the estimate you originally developed.

Labor: It's not too difficult for a skilled estimator to come close on the actual cost of materials. The problem is in estimating labor where significant deviations are usually found. To calculate labor in your cost accounting, you must know your shop-charge, labor-burden, and overhead percentages. Improper estimates of labor will also affect the amount to be allocated to overhead expense, since overhead should be calculated as a percentage of labor. Therefore, the greater the error in estimating labor, the greater the error in overhead and the less money you'll make. Or worse yet—the more money you'll lose!

If you were to use the same employees for all jobs, and the type of work remained the same, you could arrive at a close comparison between estimated and actual hours. However, an estimate on a changing labor force with different types of work will not be consistent. When this is the case (the usual pattern in contracting companies), you can significantly improve the accuracy of your estimates by basing your labor estimates on labor-units.

These additional factors are discussed later under "Labor-Units." Once you've established the labor-unit for **each item**, it will remain constant on all estimates. You can make adjustments through percentage changes to compensate for changes in productivity, weather factors, etc. Keep accurate records for labor hours (actual) per phase (slab, rough, trim, final, etc.) as you go along. It's too late to do this at the end of a job.

Job Expenses: Basically, job expenses are the costs of doing a contracting job that do not include material or labor that is incorporated into the actual work.

Permits are an example, as well as financing costs and special job insurance cost. Using an approximate or average figure in your estimate for permits may be dangerous for a job in an area you are not familiar with. Each municipality uses its own formula for determining the cost of the permit—by the job, or by amperage, by the square footage, or other factors. Check with the permit office instead of guessing. Work within your trade association to try to standardize the permit fees to eliminate doubt and confusion.

Government quotation requests limit the percentage of overhead that may be applied to an estimate, and limits the percentage of profit that can be added on. In such circumstances certain overhead expenses, such as the cost of tools, become a job expense instead of over-head. So does supervisory labor and equipment rentals. As an aid in determining assignment of specific cost to overhead or job cost, one need only to ask—if it were not for this job, would we have incurred this expense?

Estimating Procedures
Note: The subject of estimating is discussed thoroughly in a separate course with an accompanying workbook and DVDs. This course will take you through the estimating process step-by-step and complete a bid. It also includes discussions on manual versus computerized estimating.

Profit: Determining what profit to add to an estimate is influenced by various factors. How many contractors are bidding? Studies show that if four contractors bid on a job, a median profit is established. When only one contractor submits a bid, the cost average is 135 percent above average and as the quantity of contractor bids increase the average bid price decreases to about 90 percent of average when there are ten competitors. Don't feel guilty about earning excess profit on a job because the time will come when you will have to settle for minimum profit.

Some of the common variations in profit are cyclical, depending on season, business conditions, availability of money and other factors. If you need the job to keep your work force intact, or to meet a sales goal, management may elect to quote at a reduced profit. Normally, extra billing will contribute to your overhead base. At all times (but particularly when business is slow), try to upgrade a job. How about recommending paddle fans, 3-way switches, fire and burglar alarms, or other improvements that will build up your profit? Remember, jobs are commonly competitively bid.

Change Orders: Additions and change orders are negotiated, typically at a better profit margin. When changes are ordered on a job, prepare a separate estimate, and bill for it separately. Your productivity decreases on change orders, so estimate accordingly. Add additional amounts for negotiation, office labor and billing. Consider stating in your contract that a minimum flat fee will be charged for all change orders.

Inflation: Unless you take steps to compensate for inflation, you may experience a serious erosion of your profits. If you're bidding on a job that will not be completed or paid for several months, you should add a percentage to your total price that will restore the eroded value of your dollars. If you anticipate inflation to rise six percent this year (or one-half percent per month), and you don't expect payment to be made for five months, add two and one-half percent to the bid price. Why allow your customers to pay you in dollars that are cheaper than what you had to pay to do the job?

Overhead: Overhead is the cost of doing business that is not chargeable directly to any particular job. Each contracted job must pay a share of your overhead, and the most equitable way is for you to know what the percentage of overhead cost is attributable to the labor cost, then adding this percentage to each hour of labor. Part of the overhead is variable, and increases with each hour of labor that is performed. The larger part is fixed, and remains constant regardless of how much labor is done. Therefore, an incentive to the manager is to increase the amount of billable labor without radical change in the company that will increase fixed overhead. The end result is a lower percentage of overhead per hour of labor, and more competitive billing.

Retainage Cost: Some jobs require that a portion of each payment (typically 10 percent) be held for a specific period of time (typically 90 to 180 days) after the final electrical inspection; and some require a portion be held for the duration of your warrantee period.

The purpose of the owner holding back the money (Retainage) is to guarantee that the electrical system has been installed correctly and according to the contract before all final payments have been released. You might want to add the cost of money you do not have access to.

Example: Retainage cost (10%) for 180 days for a $250k project will be $1,500 at an interest rate of 12%.

Cost = ($250,000 x 10%) x (12% x 0.50)
Cost = ($25,000) x (6%)
Cost = $1,500 or 0.6% of the selling price

Expansion: Expansion results in more employees. Every time you add an employee, your variable overhead increases but your fixed overhead remains relatively constant. The result is that companies with more employees have a smaller overhead percentage per employee than smaller ones.

Prepare your job-costing analysis on a monthly basis. Use proper forms for clarity, consistency and accuracy. You'll have the records needed to review the performance of your employees, suppliers, and estimating. If the actual costs versus estimating costs are out-of-line, determine the root causes and take steps now to correct these same potential discrepancies on future estimates. Improve your personal estimating skills, and give direction to your employees. Work toward reaching your profit goals through the production of accurate job-cost estimates. An estimate is the foundation for the management of the project. When properly estimated, it can still be improperly managed. It takes both accurate estimates and good project management to make a profit.

Related Topics:
- Profit
- Labor-Units
- Markup
- Estimating

Job Costing (Estimating Analysis)

Rate Importance	minus	My Skill Level	equals	Gap
1 2 3 4 5 6 7 8 9 10	–	1 2 3 4 5 6 7 8 9 10	=	_____

Things I'm doing right: _____

_____

_____

_____

What goals can I set to improve in this area? _____

_____

_____

_____

Specific steps that I must take to achieve my improvement goals: ____

_____

_____

_____

_____

Action plan: _____

_____

_____

_____

_____

_____

When I want to complete this: _____

_____

Markup

Don't confuse markup % with profit %. Your **profit is a percentage of the selling price**, not a markup on the cost.

Calculating Profit

Only once you have estimated your break-even costs, can you determine the 'Selling Price' for a job. Use the following formula to calculate your selling price based on desired profit %:

Selling Price = Break-Even Cost/(100%-Profit%)

Example: If the break-even cost of a job is $100,000 and your desired profit is 15% of selling price:

To get 15% profit on a job that has a break-even cost of $100,000, you must divide $100,000 by (100%-15%) or $100,000/.85 to determine the selling price of $117,650.

Break-Even	$100,000—85%
Profit	$ 17,650—15%
Selling Price	$117,650—100%

There is a "short cut" to work it out:

For a five percent profit, divide the cost price by 0.95, which is (100-5)/100
For a ten percent profit, divide the cost price by 0.9
For a fifteen percent profit, divide the cost price by 0.85
For a twenty percent profit, divide the cost price by 0.8, and so on.

Do not increase your cost price by 15%. If you did this, your markup on cost would be 15%, but you would only be getting 13% profit on your selling price, as illustrated below:

Break-Even	$100,000—87%
Profit	$ 15,000—13%
Selling Price	$115,000—100%

By using the formula correctly, you will see that a profit of 15% of the selling price is greater than a 15% markup on cost.

Markup

Rate Importance	minus	My Skill Level	equals	Gap
1 2 3 4 5 6 7 8 9 10	–	1 2 3 4 5 6 7 8 9 10	=	_____

Things I'm doing right: _____

_____

_____

_____

What goals can I set to improve in this area? _____

_____

_____

_____

Specific steps that I must take to achieve my improvement goals: _____

_____

_____

_____

_____

Action plan: _____

_____

_____

_____

_____

When I want to complete this: _____

_____

Payment Schedule

The contract for every job you take on should include a payment schedule; that is, a net amount or percentage of the total price that you receive as a draw in advance, or upon billing for each milestone of the job's progress, such as slab, rough, trim, etc.

If you estimate by computer, you should know more accurately the cost for each increment of job progress, so you're aware of what your draw should be. With manual estimating, you probably have a set formula, perhaps 50 percent for slab, 30 percent for rough, and 20 percent for trim. Be cautious under this arrangement since the draws you get for the early stages may be more than your actual costs, resulting in later stages being under-billed in relation to incurred cost.

While it is great to receive all of your money up front, your billings should closely agree with the actual current cost. You don't know if you're making money when current period billings do not reflect current period cost. Your (apparently healthy) bank balance may cause you to overspend, resulting in cash-flow shortages during the latter stages of the job.

Be sure that your draws are billed correctly so that your expenses do not exceed your income in any billing period. Keep track of how much you're billing in advance. You can control cash flow by manipulating the material order schedules.

Related Topics:
• Budgeting

Payment Schedule

Rate Importance	minus	My Skill Level	equals	Gap
1 2 3 4 5 6 7 8 9 10	−	1 2 3 4 5 6 7 8 9 10	=	_____

Things I'm doing right: _____

_____

_____

What goals can I set to improve in this area? _____

_____

_____

Specific steps that I must take to achieve my improvement goals: _____

_____

_____

_____

Action plan: _____

_____

_____

_____

_____

When I want to complete this: _____

_____

Profit

Net profit is the bottom line—it's your report card! A responsible estimate will include a reasonable amount for profit. If your estimate is complete and you manage your company efficiently, you don't need much profit to stay in business. In a normal business climate, a reasonable profit margin would be between 10—30 percent of break-even cost, but in today's market, this may not be realistic.

- Strive for profit, not sales volume
- Evaluate the risk involved
- Increase profits by increasing efficiency, not by increasing prices

Let's review some factors that have a significant impact upon the achievement of profit, and what you can do to ensure that you are profitable.

Factors essential to achieve profit:

- Be confident that you are entitled to make money on EVERY job.
- Maintain control of all jobs particularly labor hours/cost, overhead, and higher priced materials.
- Motivate your employees to be efficient so that the company is profitable; this ensures that they have a job.
- Plan to make a profit by building it into the Bid.
- Establish a collection procedure, and be sure you ALWAYS get paid.
- Establish a fair price, stick to it, and sell your price!
- Increase your profit margins by increasing efficiency, not by increasing your prices.
- Maintain a consistent sales effort, to ensure that you have a greater opportunity to get the profit margin you desire.
- Be organized at all levels of business, this includes all employees.
- Commit to be profitable on every job.
- Don't meet the competition on price; sell the job at your price.
- Maintain a consistent training program to ensure your employees are efficient and are working as a team.
- Understand markup, we'll discuss this at another time.
- When you bid a job, evaluate the risk involved and adjust your profit accordingly.

Related Topics:
- Job Costing
- Markup
- Sales & Customer Service
- Billing & Collections
- Hiring & Training
- Motivating

Profitability has several added benefits besides the obvious. It will help you establish bank credit and give your employees confidence that they will have a job in the future.

The economy is always cyclical, and you will not make money every year, so you need to build up your financial reserves to offset the financial losses that will occur during the bad years. If you have not done this in the past, now would be a good time to start.

Profit

Rate Importance	minus	My Skill Level	equals	Gap
1 2 3 4 5 6 7 8 9 10	–	1 2 3 4 5 6 7 8 9 10	=	_____

Things I'm doing right: _____

_____

_____

What goals can I set to improve in this area? _____

_____

_____

Specific steps that I must take to achieve my improvement goals: _____

_____

_____

_____

Action plan: _____

_____

_____

_____

_____

When I want to complete this: _____

Record Keeping

You can keep records with a physical filing system but you can eliminate much of the paperwork by using electronic filing. Don't spend unnecessary time scanning documents just for the sake of keeping them on your computer, but when you have communication by email with documents attached, you should store those on the computer. Be sure to create a directory and file structure for the folders so that others in your office know where to find them. In some instances you just might find it more efficient to keep all your paperwork in the filing cabinets, filed by project.

Among the many records to be maintained are time cards, proposals, estimates, job-costing analyses, contracts, permits, tax records, payroll records, inventory, tool locations, and truck costs. Some of your records are required to be maintained for specific periods by various governmental agencies, such as the IRS. Your CPA can provide you with a listing of records and their retention periods.

Your bookkeeping system and the specific records it maintains will often be established for the primary purpose of paying taxes and complying with governmental mandates, none of which are intended to help you manage your business for profit.

Your accounting system must be constructed to provide not only tax and mandated data, but financial management data as well. Remember, you're not in business to pay taxes—you pay taxes because you're in business! You're going to be required to pay some taxes whether you make money or not. You're in business to make a profit, not to pay taxes. Learn the difference between a bookkeeper, a CPA, a tax advisor, and a tax attorney. Learn the difference between tax evasion and tax avoidance. One is legal—the other is not! Tax avoidance is professional management in action.

Truck records should include operating, maintenance and repair costs. You can make accurate decisions about replacing trucks only when the cost of operating an older truck, including maintenance, exceeds the cost of payments or leasing on a new truck. A factor that contractors many times fail to include in determining truck costs is the lost time for labor when a truck is unavailable due to repairs or service.

Related Topics:
- Accounting
- Budgeting

Record Keeping

Rate Importance	minus	My Skill Level	equals	Gap
1 2 3 4 5 6 7 8 9 10	−	1 2 3 4 5 6 7 8 9 10	=	_____

Things I'm doing right: _____

_____

_____

_____

What goals can I set to improve in this area? _____

_____

_____

_____

_____

Specific steps that I must take to achieve my improvement goals: _____

_____

_____

_____

_____

_____

Action plan: _____

_____

_____

_____

_____

_____

_____

When I want to complete this: _____

Selling the Job at Your Price

Selling begins when the customer says "NO." The manager or the estimator who delivers the proposal to the prospect for consideration must be sales minded. Don't lose a job because of price. Learn to overcome objections. Use the most important word in the salesman's vocabulary by asking "why?" If you know why they won't sign, concentrate your sales efforts to overcome the objection. Remember these steps in the sales presentation:

- **Attention**—get it.
- **Desire**—create it.
- **Action**—get them to say yes, ask for the order, and close the sale. It's amazing how many times sales personnel fail to ask for the order in a sales presentation.

You have many other selling points to offer. Stress your record of service and follow-up, the reputation and dependability of your company, and your liberal credit or warranty terms. Refer them to some of your satisfied customers. Be prepared to negotiate price, but not to the point where the job is financially unattractive, if not downright risky. Try to get the order confirmed in writing then and there (the first time you call), before a competitor has the opportunity to convince them that they're making the incorrect decision. Be sure to follow-up. We're all subject to moments of doubt that we've made the correct decision. A phone call in an assuring tone helps us calm our fears, and dim the voices of doom from competitors.

To keep your shop busy, you may sometimes have to accept work at prices below your regular profit. Concentrate on developing and maintaining a backlog of profitable work. The bottom line on your statement of operations (income statement) at the end of the year will tell you how successful you've been in not only getting the proper sales mix, but managing it as well. Remember that the end-of-the-year statements are just that—it's too late to change things! You must keep up with the current condition on a day-to-day basis of your business.

Aggressive companies can get leads by contacting federal, state, county and city purchasing agents, and asking to be placed on their approved bidding lists. Also, contact the government departments that handle construction and maintenance for bridges, parks, roads, schools, prisons, and hospitals. Before placing you on the bid lists, these agencies will usually check to see whether your company is bondable, and will require your meeting their financial and credit standards. Government work is usually awarded on a price basis. Purchasing agents must be very careful not to bypass the low bidder, since they must show ample justification. Government agencies pay slowly so be prepared for financing and retainage costs, and unique billing requirements. Historically Underutilized Businesses (HUB) are given some consideration not totally based upon price. When you're provided with a competitive advantage, to not use it would be wasteful.

Read books on sales techniques. Listen to tapes. Attend seminars. Take on-line courses. Discuss selling techniques at your trade association meetings. Why not show your customers

Related Topics:
- "No"—The Most Difficult Word
- Marketing vs. Selling
- Profit

how you arrived at your price, and let them see how reasonable your profit is? Give them a bid as per plans for the lowest possible price and, if you get the job, then is the time to sell them on value added extras.

Don't waste your valuable sales time. Be selective in screening out the leads. Target your efforts where you'll have the best chance of getting the business you want at a fair profit.

Selling the Job at Your Price

Rate Importance	minus	My Skill Level	equals	Gap
1 2 3 4 5 6 7 8 9 10	−	1 2 3 4 5 6 7 8 9 10	=	_____

Things I'm doing right: _____

_____

_____

_____

What goals can I set to improve in this area? _____

_____

_____

_____

Specific steps that I must take to achieve my improvement goals: _____

_____

_____

_____

_____

Action plan: _____

_____

_____

_____

_____

_____

When I want to complete this: _____

_____

Service and/or Shop Charge Determinations

Labor costs are broken down into fieldwork (which you'll bill for), and shop time (which is part of overhead). Your profit picture will be adversely affected by dead time due to bad planning and scheduling. For example, not having the proper materials on hand when and where needed, not having tools at the jobsite on time, by truck breakdowns, and weather-related events.

Make it a habit to log nonproductive hours. What happens if you run ten hours over on a job because there is a problem with material delivery or other subcontractor delays? Everything has to be allocated to a specific area (shop time for example). Such records can be used in negotiations with suppliers, and support for extra billings or change orders. Purchasing, scheduling and supervisory personnel must be aware of just how much time is truly of the essence. Remember the old saw—that which is not measured will not be improved!

Tell your staff that anytime someone else causes a problem, which in turn causes you a delay, you will list the hours on their timecard as shop time, and explain why. Tell them to be specific—no generator, no plans, no material, clean up site after subcontractor (who worked before), etc. The more you let them know that time is important to you, the more important it will become to them.

If there is a problem in the field, log the time as shop time. You can track the number of hours in lost time for specific reasons. Determine if a change is cost-effective, or if the cure would be more expensive than the loss.

Service and/or Shop Charge Determinations

Rate Importance	minus	My Skill Level	equals	Gap
1 2 3 4 5 6 7 8 9 10	–	1 2 3 4 5 6 7 8 9 10	=	_____

Things I'm doing right: _____

_____

_____

What goals can I set to improve in this area? _____

_____

_____

Specific steps that I must take to achieve my improvement goals: _____

_____

_____

_____

Action plan: _____

_____

_____

_____

_____

When I want to complete this: _____

_____

Taxes

As you accumulate FICA and payroll-withholding taxes, consider depositing them on a monthly basis into an interest-bearing savings account. When you pay them quarterly, the interest represents additional company income. Keep money working for you as long as you can.

Recognize your responsibilities. If the general contractor does not cover your employees for workers' compensation, you must do it. Sign an agreement with each of them, and with any other employee you use to assure them that they'll have all the insurance coverage the law requires. Report their earnings on Tax Form 1099.

The following list includes some of the forms you should be familiar with:

- IRS Forms: W-2, W-4, 941, UTC-6
- Tax Payments and Due Dates, Penalty Charges
- Federal Unemployment, FICA, and Withholding
- State Unemployment, FICA, Withholding, Sales Taxes
- Vehicle Tags

Taxes

Rate Importance	minus	My Skill Level	equals	Gap
1 2 3 4 5 6 7 8 9 10	–	1 2 3 4 5 6 7 8 9 10	=	_____

Things I'm doing right: _____

_____

_____

What goals can I set to improve in this area? _____

_____

_____

Specific steps that I must take to achieve my improvement goals: _____

_____

_____

_____

Action plan: _____

_____

_____

_____

When I want to complete this: _____

_____

Notes

Chapter

Job Management (Project)

Proper job management requires much more than supervision of employees. You must remain aware of all factors concerned with on-the-job performance. This means having the proper materials and tools on-site or in inventory, knowing the proper amount of inventory to carry, familiarizing yourself with local codes, developing relationships with inspectors, and much more.

This portion of the Business Management Workbook will take you step-by-step through critical areas of job management. By reading and studying this chapter, you're taking the first and most important step in becoming effective at job management.

Training is critical, not only for you but your staff members as well. Plan to use training facilities in your organization and outside educational sources to prepare yourself and your employees for more responsibilities and greater earning opportunities.

If no in-house training is now in effect, plan to begin a program of continuing education as soon as possible. Training your employees in current methods and the use of new materials will result in higher proficiency. Training should include consistent adherence to safety standards. Consistency and well-trained personnel will ultimately result in an organization that is finely tuned to current trends with proven track records of safety and profit.

Remember that quality job management also involves directing your employees through delegation of responsibility and accountability, and identification of corporate goals and duties.

Chapter 3—Job Management (Project)
Table of Contents

Bid Analysis

Reduce or eliminate potentially costly mistakes on future bids by researching the factors involved in the development of bid estimates. Make reasonable adjustments for variable factors, such as overly aggressive deadlines, extreme weather conditions, and timely availability of materials, trained crewmembers, and other subcontractors.

Establish a procedure whereby copies of all bids prepared in the past (and all future bids) are retained in a central reference file or electronic database. You can use this information to compare past performance and expedite the preparation of future similar bids.

Research the performance history of other subcontractors who will be working on the project before you. By knowing the performance histories of these subcontractors, you can be prepared for possible time delays due to the need for additional cleanup, extra materials required, enhanced supervisory efforts, etc. This information will allow you to prepare a future bid more effectively and profitably. It can also alert you to potential losses in current jobs in progress.

Related Topics:
- Estimating Procedures

Bid Analysis

Rate Importance	minus	My Skill Level	equals	Gap
1 2 3 4 5 6 7 8 9 10	–	1 2 3 4 5 6 7 8 9 10	=	_____

Things I'm doing right: _____

_____

_____

_____

What goals can I set to improve in this area? _____

_____

_____

_____

Specific steps that I must take to achieve my improvement goals: _____

_____

_____

_____

_____

Action plan: _____

_____

_____

_____

_____

When I want to complete this: _____

_____

Change Orders (Extras)

Every job you take on should have a written contract, limiting your responsibilities and outlining the parameters of the job. However, jobs are rarely completed exactly as originally planned. All changes, extras, deviations, amendments, expansions and variations to the job as originally specified in the contract should be executed in writing by a change order, and reference should be made to the original contract as being part of the overall job.

Each change must be fully understood by both the customer and the contractor to eliminate future misunderstanding. Difficulties arise in collecting on change orders because there's a question about who ordered the change and lack of an authorized signature. If the general contractor's foreman or supervisor is so authorized, they should have change order forms available at the jobsite, and submit one to the contractor before any of the changes are started.

It is important that all construction personnel comply with all company policies, and that includes change orders. Be sure to explain the policy thoroughly and clear up any misunderstanding before sending individuals out in the field. Also, be sure to provide this information to any new employees so that you can be assured that company policy is adhered to consistently.

From the start, state that you bill for change orders immediately and that you COLLECT for change orders. If a customer requests additional work and there's a balance due, notify them that no service or warranty work and no change orders will be completed until the balance is paid in full. To reduce collection difficulties, get in writing ahead of time, the name of the person(s) who can authorize change orders, and clarify the timetable for billing. It is poor policy to wait until the contract is completed before billing the customer for changes and extras. At that time, details may not be as clear. Invoice and get paid for extras as soon as they are completed.

Remember that change orders cost more money in labor and material. Don't ballpark your quote. It's better to submit a price after a couple of hours or the next day before submitting a quote that will be wrong.

Charging on a basis of time and material reduces the incentive of the contractor to increase efficiency and thereby increase profit on these revisions. It's more profitable to furnish an estimate, and use it as a goal to improve upon. If your company is weak in the field of estimating, consider taking our estimating course.

Change orders are a normal part of the construction business and you should anticipate them. If someone wants a change that is unnecessary, make sure that your profits are high enough to compensate for all of your costs involved in making this change - see how badly they really want it. Remember though, that Change Orders are not a license to steal from the owner. Fair compensation is due, but gouging can turn a good job into a litigation nightmare, and your reputation as an honest contractor into something else.

Understand the basic dynamics of the construction industry—jobs are competitively bid, and change orders are negotiated. Profits from bid jobs are always under pressure from the start due to both good, professionally managed companies, and from not so well managed companies. Ballpark bidding, hasty estimating, and a general lack of reading and understanding the bid documents will cost you money.

Bid reserves for unseen contingencies can no longer be counted upon to make good a bad bid. The job-cost estimate was (or should have been) specifically for what was called for by the contract documents, not what someone (now that the project is underway) wants. Businesses today cannot absorb extra work in the hope of getting more work from a customer in the future. When pricing change orders, do a full-cost analysis, not a quick, about, around, last time it cost, best guess.

Supervision of construction projects includes the management of field change orders. Change disrupts the plan that has been developed for the project. It delays execution, delays parts delivery, and it tends to paralyze the workers. Change orders must include all costs associated with the disruption of the flow, rhythm and profitable management of the work progress.

On occasion, you may find yourself having to negotiate the pricing of change orders. Be sure that if your company is going to be forced into a negotiation, that you have a fighter in the ring. Not everyone is well suited for the task of negotiating change orders. Keep field personnel's attention focused on building the job by having others prepare and negotiate change orders. Consider sending key personnel to special role-playing type negotiation and negotiating strategy seminars.

Related Topics:
- Contracts
- Job-Costing (Estimating Analysis)
- Estimating

Change Orders (Extras)

Rate Importance	minus	My Skill Level	equals	Gap
1 2 3 4 5 6 7 8 9 10	–	1 2 3 4 5 6 7 8 9 10	=	_____

Things I'm doing right: _____

_____

_____

What goals can I set to improve in this area? _____.

_____

_____

Specific steps that I must take to achieve my improvement goals: _____

_____

_____

_____

Action plan: _____

_____

_____

_____

_____

When I want to complete this: _____

_____

Codes and Standards

Occasionally, you'll find yourself at the mercy of the local inspector on any contracting job that you do.

- Make the investment in training time for you, your supervisors, and estimators to become knowledgeable in the local codes.
- Make it a policy to adhere to plans.
- Obtain all required permits.
- Establish a professional working relationship with the inspectors in the areas where you do repeat work. Know their individual areas of enhanced inspections, learn what they like to see most on jobs, and what they think is most (and least) important. If you anticipate problems with an inspector on a particular job that may cost you money, adjust your estimate to compensate.
- You must be knowledgeable about the building codes in each geographic area where you do business. Ignorance or misinterpretation of code requirements can be costly. If you're not sure of code requirements in any aspect of the job, investigate. Repeated violations in adhering to code in an industry where you make your living are inexcusable. Know the licensing, insurance and permitting requirements of the state (and county) in which you operate your business. Not knowing can be expensive, and not complying can be more expensive.

There are seminars offered regularly on changes in the *National Electrical Code®* (*NEC®*), local codes and other information relevant to your business or industry. Many are sponsored by organizations that have the information needed quickly and are prepared to share it with you effectively. Maintain an awareness of all building code changes as they affect your business.

Safety standards are as important as building codes in many types of work. If your firm works in classified hazardous areas, from elevated heights, or makes use of construction cranes, you need to keep up-to-date on the Occupational Safety & Health Administration's (OSHA) construction safety standards. When your firm is heavily engaged in maintenance-type activities, other standards such as the National Fire Protection Agency (NFPA®) 70E® and NFPA 101® should be on your supervisor's training plans. When accidents occur, OSHA fines are just the beginning of your legal troubles. Develop and see that your firm's safety policy is not just given lip service, but also truly complied with.

Codes and Standards

Rate Importance	minus	My Skill Level	equals	Gap
1 2 3 4 5 6 7 8 9 10	–	1 2 3 4 5 6 7 8 9 10	=	_____

Things I'm doing right: _____

_____

_____

What goals can I set to improve in this area? _____

_____

_____

Specific steps that I must take to achieve my improvement goals: _____

_____

_____

_____

Action plan: _____

_____

_____

_____

_____

When I want to complete this: _____

_____

Cost Overrun

Who is at fault? Management is inclined to blame labor, since the cost of materials can usually be estimated with a more consistent degree of accuracy than labor. Experience indicates that there are two common sources of major labor cost deviations, both of which can be corrected by management action.

Poor estimating. Without having the historical data available on previous jobs of a similar nature, accurate estimation of field labor cost is difficult. It follows that if this type of job is one that your company is inexperienced in doing, your risk is greater, and you should include a greater profit margin in your estimates to cover possible contingencies.

Poor scheduling. Not having the right materials, the right tools, the right information, the right training, and the right people, all at the right place at the right time. All of these responsibilities are those of management. That's a pretty tall order, isn't it? Don't worry; we all know that we work in an imperfect world so no one should expect perfection from you. Nevertheless, this is what you should work for.

Sometimes, in spite of your best efforts, causes of overruns are out of your control. Your field employees may be held up while waiting for other subcontractors to finish their work so that you can get in. Bad weather or other intangibles may hold you up unexpectedly.

Consider whether you may have picked the wrong customer, or picked a job you weren't skilled to do. This type of job takes too much time and increases labor-units on a job. Place employees in a position where they can do a job without requiring additional on-the-job training. Train your unskilled labor and provide better supervision. Be sure to have the proper tools on the job. Unexpected problems may be due to a bad estimate.

Do YOU schedule work or do you allow your CUSTOMERS to schedule work? Do you attend or participate in pre-construction meetings?

Order materials in advance so they arrive in accordance with the construction schedule. When schedules are changed, immediately check to see if material deliveries can comply with the new project schedule. This keeps your crew from standing around waiting for material.

The end result of cost overruns is a reduction in profits and upsets in cash flow. Management can help make your contracts more profitable by providing education and licensing opportunities to employees, which makes them more organized and efficient. It's also better practice for a contractor to advance and promote employees within the organization, rather than hire from the outside.

The quality of your work as well as the quality of your equipment and materials is another consideration. If you order and use poor quality materials or equipment not specified in the contract, you might be required to replace them with better quality materials. And when you're using poor quality or inexperienced personnel in the job, you might be required to re-do the work. This could be a significant cause for cost overruns.

What else can you do to reduce cost overruns? Start with overhauling office and management procedures. Reevaluate estimating skills of your personnel and learn how to assign labor-units more accurately. Understand overhead, and why percentages don't always work. Make sure your markup reflects the amount of risk entailed in each job.

No matter what the specific cause of cost overruns is, the responsibility always falls to management. You can delegate authority, but not responsibility!

Related Topics:
- Job-Costing
- Markup
- Estimating Procedures
- Labor-Units
- Inventory

Cost Overrun

Rate Importance	minus	My Skill Level	equals	Gap
1 2 3 4 5 6 7 8 9 10	–	1 2 3 4 5 6 7 8 9 10	=	_____

Things I'm doing right: _____

_____

_____

_____

What goals can I set to improve in this area? _____

_____

_____

_____

Specific steps that I must take to achieve my improvement goals: _____

_____

_____

_____

_____

Action plan: _____

_____

_____

_____

_____

_____

When I want to complete this: _____

_____

Estimating vs. Bidding

A good percentage of work is acquired through the estimating process, and most jobs are awarded to the contractor who has the best-perceived price, but not necessarily the lowest. Because of the demands to have the best-perceived price, profit margins are limited. This permits you to have only a small margin for error in the estimate. A proper estimate must accurately determine your cost in completing the job according to the customer's needs. This price must be acceptable to your customers at a value that includes sufficient profit for you to stay in business. In addition to helping you determine the selling price for a job, the estimate is used as the foundation for project management.

Determining the selling price for a job is actually two separate components:

- **The estimate**, which determines the cost of the job.
- **The bid**, which determines the job's selling price.

It is critical that you understand the difference between an estimated cost and a bid price. Estimating is determining your cost and bidding is determining the selling price.

The purpose of estimating is to determine the cost of a project before you actually do the work. Estimating must take into consideration variable job conditions, the cost of materials, labor cost, direct job expenses, and management costs (overhead). Once you know the estimated cost of a project, you can determine the selling price of the job. Determining the selling price of a job is called bidding.

There are several types of bid requirements that you might experience. They include:

- Competitive bid
- Design build
- Negotiated work
- Time and material (fixed fee)
- Unit pricing

Competitive Bid—This type of bid can be for private, public, or government projects. These projects can be found in the newspapers in the classified section under Public Notices, as well as trade publications. These publications list projects by category (such as residential, industrial, commercial), and by total expected project price range.

Design Build—Sometimes an electrical contractor is given a general floor layout without much detail and requested to design and construct the electrical wiring according to written specifications. To be successful with design build, you really need to know your customers' needs and the electrical *Code*.

Negotiated Work—Negotiated work is generally not advertised and there are a limited number of contractors requested to negotiate the bid price. The contractor and the customer negotiate a price that satisfies both parties.

Note: The subject of estimating is discussed thoroughly in a separate course with an accompanying workbook and DVDs. This course will take you through the estimating process step-by-step and complete a bid. It also includes discussions on manual versus computerized estimating. For more information visit www.mikeholt.com.

Time and Material or Fixed Fee Proposal—Time and material pricing, sometimes called *fixed fee*, is required when existing conditions make it difficult to provide a fixed dollar bid. This type of bid is based on a given rate-per-hour for labor (including benefits, overhead and profit) with the material billed separately at an agreed markup, such as 20 percent above cost. A variation of the fixed fee method is a fixed lump sum price for labor only, with materials billed separately using the percentage markup.

Unit Pricing—Some jobs are awarded on a unit price basis, where the unit price includes both material and labor cost. This is often the case when the customer is not quite sure of the quantities of the specific items. Unit pricing is used for almost all types of construction, such as renovations, office build-outs, change orders, etc.

Even if the manager does not do the actual estimating, there are certain controls that he or she must exercise in determining the form the estimate takes. The draw schedule should be established so that the amount billed for any section of the job should be at least equivalent to the sums paid out. Without this safeguard, the cash flow would be negatively impaired, and unanticipated financing costs may be incurred.

A bill of materials must be prepared, and the proper amount of materials must be sent to the jobsite to cover the work to be done. Inadequate materials on hand results in unproductive time in waiting until replenishments are received. Shipping too much increases inventory shrinkages. In addition, a lot of extra material is left at the job after the work is completed. Or, if the material is gathered up and returned to the shop, nobody bothers to separate, record and properly restock it.

Don't underestimate your overhead cost by a simple arithmetic error. Overhead is a percentage of sales, not cost as some estimators believe. Estimators should also be cautioned against allocating a fixed percentage of overhead to a job. Percentages just don't work. Where a job requires more labor, more overhead must be added to the estimate than for a job with the same dollar amount, but having less labor. This is because the more billable, productive labor the estimate calls for, the more un-billable labor (or shop charge) there will be. This is dead time, which increases in proportion to productive time. You don't bill for shop time, but it increases your overhead.

Notice on your financial statement that field labor is considered a direct cost, and office labor is an overhead cost. These two types of labor should not only be kept separate, but the residual costs of labor, such as FICA, insurance, workers' compensation, etc. should also be maintained separately.

A standard estimating procedure should be established and followed on every job. Benefits of an organized, detailed and formalized job-cost estimating procedure are:

- The time required for preparation of each estimate will decrease
- The accuracy of estimates will increase
- Checking of successive estimates will be easier
- Successive estimates will be more consistent

Always include quotes, specifications and subcontracts. For increased accuracy, always use labor-units in your bids. Don't forget to research factors in the job you are bidding, particularly the variables.

Related Topics:
- Job-Costing
- Change Orders
- Estimating Procedures
- Labor-Units

Estimating vs. Bidding

Rate Importance	minus	My Skill Level	equals	Gap
1 2 3 4 5 6 7 8 9 10	–	1 2 3 4 5 6 7 8 9 10	=	_____

Things I'm doing right: _____

_____

_____

_____

What goals can I set to improve in this area? _____

_____

_____

Specific steps that I must take to achieve my improvement goals: _____

_____

_____

_____

Action plan: _____

_____

_____

_____

_____

When I want to complete this: _____

_____

Estimating Process

Before you begin the estimate, you must understand the scope of work to be completed according to the contract. To accomplish this, you must have all of the information about the job and a current set of blueprints and specifications.

While the duties of estimators may vary from contractor to contractor, the basic principles remain the same. The system must be efficient, accurate and attempt to prevent common mistakes. Generally, the duties of the estimator include but are not limited to the following:

- Determining the cost of the job (estimate)
- Purchasing material
- Ensuring bid accuracy
- Project management/tracking

A good estimator is identified by:

- A willingness to learn.
- A good knowledge of construction and the ability to visualize specific requirements.
- An orderly mind and a tendency to be careful, accurate, and neat.
- An open mind willing to change and take advantage of new products and new technology.
- Decisiveness and the ability to make decisions and not be intimidated by details.
- Fairness, honesty and integrity.
- Knowledge of applicable codes and the ability to read blueprints.
- Patience—you must be able to finish the estimate without losing your cool.
- Procedures and the ability to follow them.

There are three primary methods of estimating a job:

- The manual method
- Computer-assisted method
- Estimating service

Each method has its own set of advantages and disadvantages. You need to be honest and select the method that works best for you. Once you understand manual estimating, you can determine which method is the most cost effective for you.

Manual Estimates—Even though manual estimates are good for very small projects, especially if you use unit pricing, and have been sufficient for electrical contractors for over a hundred years, this method is not efficient for the electrical contractor who is regularly bidding jobs. Because it takes so much time to estimate a job manually, you have only enough time to get the bottom line price and not much more. Manual estimating requires so much time that estimates often become backlogged and project management suffers. Today, more than any other time in history, we operate in an age of instant information and expected response. Few customers are willing to give you the time you need to prepare an accurate manual bid.

Estimating Software—The computer-assisted method of estimating is actually the same as estimating manually, except that a computer is used to perform the thousands of mathematical calculations millions of times faster and more accurately than a human. The margin for error when using a computer is reduced significantly. Your bids will become clearer, more legible, and professional in appearance. And you can reduce your estimating time by as much as 75 percent.

Estimating Service—An estimating service is a temporary agency that you only pay for when you need it. You might use it to double-check a bid, or if you don't have the time to do the bid yourself. It's an excellent tool to help you gain estimating experience at a reduced risk. And, you can enjoy the benefits of computer-generated estimates without investing in your own computer estimating system. Estimating service fees are generally based on the total bid dollar amount.

Not all expenses can be anticipated in advance, but experienced estimators accept a satisfactory margin of error in the accuracy of the bid. If you break the job down into its smallest possible parts, then the magnitude of each mistake will be reduced, and hopefully the mistakes will cancel each other out.

An accurate estimate must include labor cost including burden (fringes), material cost including fixture and switchgear quotes, sales tax, subcontract and rental expenses, direct job expenses, and overhead. To determine the bid price, always include a margin for profit.

The following is a step-by-step procedure for processing a job-cost estimate that has proven its worth on countless jobs over several years:

1. Register job (name, address, phone, etc.)
2. Study plans and review specifications.
   a. Site Plans
   b. Architectural
   c. Structural
   d. Mechanical
3. Determine approach to take-off.
4. Count, measure and list all items.
5. Write up.
6. Recheck.
7. Price, extend and subtotal.
8. Transfer subtotals to bid summary.
9. Apply overhead and profit.
10. Make necessary adjustments.
11. Total bid summary, and have it checked.

Reasons for errors:

a. Hurry—too little time allowed.

b. Improper estimating forms.

c. Failure to read specifications and plans.

d. Inaccurate or incomplete determination of jobsite conditions.

Results of error:

a. Omit section of job.

b. Forget to include special equipment.

c. Forget to include quotes.

d. Forget labor, job expense, and overhead.

e. Forget typical floor.

f. Assume all floors to be the same.

g. Assume standard grade devices are acceptable.

h. Failure to include outside or underground work equipment or connection.

i. Forget changes to original specifications, plans.

j. Incorrect extensions.

k. Errors in multiplication or addition.

l. Using wholesale take-offs.

You should:

a. Read every word of specifications.

b. Study and check all plans.

c. Clear up any doubts.

d. Don't estimate when you are rushed or tired.

e. Refuse to enter bid not properly prepared.

f. Check all quantities, price and extensions.

g. Estimate in an orderly sequence.

h. Use proper forms.

Related Topics:

• Job-Costing

• Estimating vs. Bidding

Estimating Process

Rate Importance	minus	My Skill Level	equals	Gap
1 2 3 4 5 6 7 8 9 10	–	1 2 3 4 5 6 7 8 9 10	=	_____

Things I'm doing right: _____

_____

_____

_____

What goals can I set to improve in this area? _____

_____

_____

_____

Specific steps that I must take to achieve my improvement goals: _____

_____

_____

_____

_____

Action plan: _____

_____

_____

_____

_____

When I want to complete this: _____

_____

Inventory

Your inventory could conceivably represent more than 50 percent of your current assets. This is a significant amount and means that you must keep a close watch on this account. You should know whether the amount of inventory is reasonable in relation to sales and other operations of your business. Know how rapidly your inventory turns over. Be sure you're not investing in slow-moving items (six or less turns per year). Balance your material and tool purchase decisions between maintaining an adequate supply on hand against possibly losing sales due to an inadequate supply. Take action to maintain the size inventory necessary to get the job done effectively and profitably.

How large should your inventory be? If you have an efficient estimating system (particularly a computerized one), you'll maintain a very low inventory and order materials as a contract is received. Materials are to be shipped to the jobsite as each section is ready for work and in sufficient quantities for that amount of work. An added advantage to this kind of control will be less theft, waste, loss and pilferage, because you'll not be over-ordering and leaving extra materials around after the work is done.

By maintaining the lowest possible inventory, you improve cash flow. However, it's possible to affect savings by buying in truckload quantities that qualify for a discount. You may also order materials for possible future work when you have information that the price will be increased shortly. Be sure that the extra handling and storage cost over a long period of time doesn't eat up anticipated savings. Remember that low price is not everything. You'll want to develop a relationship with suppliers who will help you solve your problems and be there when you need them.

Excess inventory usually is maintained until it "ages" and the cost of storing it, moving it, and ultimately dumping it costs more than the value of the material stored. Clean up and get rid of "junk." If you don't need something, don't pay to store it. Identify your dead inventory on a regular basis. Consider the handling costs and the management costs involved in maintaining unneeded items.

Use your inventory evaluation as a measure of your ordering procedures. Determine what you ordered and what you used. If there's a discrepancy, try to determine if it's because of an incorrect ordering procedure or due to a situation beyond your control. Donating new but unneeded materials to local trade and technical schools can sometimes be used for tax and personnel recruitment advantages.

If you can handle your supplies in an orderly, effective way, you'll save a lot of hassles, and a lot of time. Your workers' attitudes will also change because when they see that you care, they'll start to care too.

Related Topics:
• Cost Overrun

Inventory

Rate Importance	minus	My Skill Level	equals	Gap
1 2 3 4 5 6 7 8 9 10	–	1 2 3 4 5 6 7 8 9 10	=	_____

Things I'm doing right: _____

_____

_____

What goals can I set to improve in this area? _____

_____

_____

Specific steps that I must take to achieve my improvement goals: _____

_____

_____

_____

Action plan: _____

_____

_____

_____

When I want to complete this: _____

_____

Job Schedule

Give adequate consideration to the amount of physical labor required for a job in determining the length of time you can realistically devote to a project. Give careful consideration to the length of the project in relation to the amount of physical labor.

Your anticipated labor requirements should be forecast at least several months in advance, or your schedule may end up in disaster. Create a projected monthly budget in labor based on the jobs that are in-house and what you expect to get. Prepare in advance what your manpower requirements will be. If you have a heavy need for a certain period of time, see that enough labor is available in time to provide training and familiarity with your firm's systems. In slow periods, try to acquire service work.

If you don't schedule your labor, you can unexpectedly run into overtime requirements that you have to pay for. Always try to work out a schedule with the general contractor where you can coordinate your own work schedule with other subcontractors. If your general contractor speeds up his completion schedule ahead of the time he originally gave you, remind him that he is responsible for overtime pay. Check the specific contract document first, as it may be your responsibility.

A time schedule, broken down by job sections, should be a part of every contract you negotiate. Any penalty clause you have to sign for running behind schedule should be balanced by an incentive clause for early completion. In any case, don't accept a clause that will penalize you for failure of other subcontractors to finish in time and leave the work area free and ready for your own crew.

Related Topics:

• Planning & Organizing

Job Schedule

Rate Importance	minus	My Skill Level	equals	Gap
1 2 3 4 5 6 7 8 9 10	−	1 2 3 4 5 6 7 8 9 10	=	_____

Things I'm doing right: _____

_____

_____

What goals can I set to improve in this area? _____

_____

_____

Specific steps that I must take to achieve my improvement goals: _____

_____

_____

_____

Action plan: _____

_____

_____

_____

_____

When I want to complete this: _____

_____

Job Selection

Before you estimate any job, you should always ask yourself—is this the most efficient use of my time, talents, and skills at this time? Because of limited resources, such as energy, time, and money, you can't estimate all jobs. You must become selective about which jobs you feel will better meet your financial goals. Look for the kind of work you can handle, in competition with companies that cannot outbid you because of their size or field of specialization. To be profitable, you need to be an efficient contractor, not the largest. Treat your employees and customers fairly and honestly. Check your labor budget to ascertain that you'll have the manpower to do the work on the anticipated schedule.

If you want to be competitive in a market you're not familiar with, find out how you can gain the needed experience. One way to gain experience is through the school of hard knocks, but maybe you can become more creative and find a way to educate yourself before you take that kind of risk. Talk to other contractors, attend seminars, read trade magazines, and watch training DVDs. Do whatever you can to reduce any kind of loss you might incur as a result of inexperience.

If you do not think you are going to make money on the job, do not bid on it. Remember why you are in business, and that it is better to be honest and up-front than to make excuses or pretend to be interested when you are not. Bidding on jobs you cannot win or on which you cannot make a profit just increases your overhead and will make you less competitive in the future.

If there's work available that you would like to qualify for, be ready the next time it's offered. Turning over dollars without expectation of profit is bad planning because you may tie yourself up when the opportunity presents itself to do the kind of work you know, and can make money on. Your only reason for being in business is to make a profit, so guide yourself in that direction. Labor has a very short shelf life; it must be used up each day.

Related Topics:
- "No"—The Most Difficult Word
- Selling The Job at Your Price

Job Selection

Rate Importance	minus	My Skill Level	equals	Gap
1 2 3 4 5 6 7 8 9 10	–	1 2 3 4 5 6 7 8 9 10	=	_____

Things I'm doing right: _____

_____

_____

What goals can I set to improve in this area? _____

_____

_____

Specific steps that I must take to achieve my improvement goals: _____

_____

_____

_____

Action plan: _____

_____

_____

_____

_____

When I want to complete this: _____

_____

Labor-Units

The calculation of labor-units is based on the assumption that a skilled and motivated contractor is completing the task under standard installation conditions with the proper tools. A labor-unit is comprised of six major components. They include:

- Installation   50%
- Job Layout   15%
- Material handling and cleanup   10%
- Nonproductive labor   5%
- Supervision   10%
- Tool handling   10%

Estimating with labor-units is both a science and an art form. It's a science in the sense that the labor required to complete a task is a function of the materials to be installed and their quantities. If you know the quantity of each material required for a job, you can easily determine the labor required. It's also an art form in the sense that you need to become creative in making some adjustments to the labor-units for the specific job conditions.

For many contractors, determining the labor for a job is often very scary and intimidating, so before you actually estimate a job, you need to gain confidence in how to determine the expected labor. There are two methods of estimating the labor for a job; one is using your experience from previous jobs, and the second is labor-units. Using your experience is fine as long as you have sufficient experience, but the most accurate and fastest way of estimating labor on a job is through the use of labor-units. With labor-units, you have a fixed base to work from (unlike experience), which is subject to mood or perception.

A labor-unit represents the total cost of labor to install an item or assembly. In the estimating take-off, you count the quantity of each item, and by multiplying by the labor-unit for that item, you come up with the labor cost to install that number of units.

When you calculate the labor-unit, the installation time is only part of it. To this figure you add the time requirement for traveling to and from jobsite, material handling and cleanup, job layout, record keeping, tool setup, plus other time-consuming activities. Consider the time spent by the supervisor for these duties and for ordering supplies, coordinating work with other trades, and time for the builder and inspector to do their jobs. Include the cost of employee's benefits.

It doesn't help you to know the labor-units of your competitors—they're not yours! To be competitive, you must develop your own labor-units and you must have information on past labor performance of similar jobs. Track job hours and compare them against the job's budgeted hours. After a while you'll gain the knowledge necessary to adjust your labor for the next job. In addition, past job performance is useful for bid analysis. If you're not accustomed to using labor-units, determine if the learning time to accustom yourself to this new method warrants the time.

There is not one set of labor-units that can be applied to all jobs. They must be increased or decreased to accommodate varying job conditions. There are many variable factors that must be taken into consideration on a per job basis: things such as weather, repetitive jobs, obstacles in work areas, rate of progress, forced interruptions, lack of materials or tools on the jobsite, delays by other contractors, the complexity of the system being installed, and mismanagement in general. Allocate a percentage of time to wasted time due to these factors.

Much time can be eliminated that would otherwise be wasted by proper training, proper ordering of materials, researching the work habits of other contractors, knowing your inspectors, etc. With experience and historical data, you'll develop techniques to help you adjust the labor-units to represent your productivity with specific job conditions.

Although it would appear that a great deal of time is spent researching the information to determine labor-units, the time is well spent. It can prevent needless delays and miscalculations in determining the labor-units and also serve to make your future bids more accurate and more competitive. The return received time and again from job to job makes the investment a very attractive one over the long term.

Related Topics:
- Job Costing
- Cost Overrun
- Service and/or Shop Charge Determinations
- Estimating vs. Bidding

Labor-Units

Rate Importance	minus	My Skill Level	equals	Gap
1 2 3 4 5 6 7 8 9 10	–	1 2 3 4 5 6 7 8 9 10	=	_____

Things I'm doing right: _____

_____

_____

What goals can I set to improve in this area? _____

_____

_____

Specific steps that I must take to achieve my improvement goals: _____

_____

_____

_____

Action plan: _____

_____

_____

_____

_____

When I want to complete this: _____

Plans

Few things can be more frustrating than to bid successfully on a set of plans, and then find an altered set supplied with the contract. Or that more than one set of plans has been distributed to the general contractor, the inspector, and various subcontractors.

Protect yourself by stating on your proposal that your estimate is in accordance with Plan No. XYZ dated XYZ. Plans can be changed without your knowing about it. Put your identifying mark or code on the set of plans you used in your estimate. Highlight the plans as you prepare your estimate. Restrict your price quotation to the original set, and increase your price if the plans are changed without your knowledge.

Do not certify that the plans will meet local code, but that the installation will. Where you possess the expertise, design build-type work typically offers a higher profit margin than plan and specification-type work. With this type of work, your firm is responsible for the completeness, and code compliance of the plans. Unless you have the required engineering design-level expertise, design build-type work should be avoided.

Related Topics:
- Estimating vs. Bidding
- Proposals

Plans

Rate Importance	minus	My Skill Level	equals	Gap
1 2 3 4 5 6 7 8 9 10	–	1 2 3 4 5 6 7 8 9 10	=	_____

Things I'm doing right: _____

_____

_____

What goals can I set to improve in this area? _____

_____

_____

Specific steps that I must take to achieve my improvement goals: _____

_____

_____

_____

Action plan: _____

_____

_____

_____

_____

When I want to complete this: _____

_____

Project Manager's Role

Not all of the following will apply to every job, but the following is an overview of the responsibilities of an Electrical Project Manager.

- Verify awarded scope of work in relation to your company's proposal quoted base cost and adders. If you were not the estimator for the awarded project, obtain copies of the project proposal and bid documents and drawings. A very important part of this package will include supplier's quotes for lighting and switch-gear packages, as well as any sub-contracted quotes for specialty systems such as data, fire alarm or nurse call systems, etc.
- Review contract before signing to ensure fair and equitable practices, and verify that the dollar amount of the contract matches your company's proposed scope of work base bid with adders.
- Prepare and file mechanic's lien on the project.
- Prepare and send to general contractor submittals for material approval by owner or architect—usually switchgear and lighting packages but larger projects may also require pipe and wire and devices. This includes contacting suppliers and verifying quotes and requesting submittal packages and cut sheets for their products.
- Prepare permit documents including a permit application to the AHJ but may also include load calculations and panel schedules, and drawings such as a one-line of the distribution system, egress lighting layout, etc.
- Obtain schedule from general contractor and determine manpower needed to complete milestone tasks on schedule.
- Once submittals have been approved by the architect or owner and have their stamp and/or signature, issue purchase orders, delivery instructions, and request estimated delivery dates. Co-ordinate the purchase and delivery dates to minimize overhead costs but still satisfy deadlines. Try to get the material billing from your supplier to be covered by your progress billing to the general contractor. Also prepare project information requested by supplier that will assist them in their job accounting and lien processing.
- Communicate to your project foreman or field personnel all pertinent information that they will need to proceed with the job, including a copy of the bid scope of work, updated construction documents such as project specifications and drawings, and the project schedule. Discuss the potential problems that you foresee and suggest possible solutions that will help complete on time and under budget. Be sure to communicate with them the details and scheduled delivery dates of the lighting and gear packages along with the specialty systems so that he will know the demands of the job. They must also have a copy of the submittals especially the material cut-sheets so that they can plan installation procedures and layout.

- Prepare and log any formal "RFIs" (Requests For Information) that you or your foreman may have for the architect or general contractor about the project.
  - Prepare formal "delay of job" letters that notify the general contractor of delays to the schedule by others that will prevent your timely completion of the project or impact costs.
  - Prepare any change order cost estimates that may be requested by the general contractor or architect. Usually, if these requests come from the architect, they will be in the form of an "ASI" (Architect's Supplemental Instruction). Log these changes along with the rejection or approval dates and revise your recorded contract amount accordingly for billing purposes.
  - Communicate approved change order details to your field personnel and discuss any scheduling challenges.
  - Receive reports from your project foreman that aid in tracking progress and costs.
  - Prepare progress billings against the contract amount. These need to include original contract amount and changes to show justification for any revisions to the contract amount.
  - Prepare the conditional and the final unconditional lien releases.
  - Prepare final closeout documents such as operating and maintenance manuals, as-built drawings, and warranty letters.
  - Prepare final cost analysis of the project for review.

Project Manager's Role

Rate Importance	minus	My Skill Level	equals	Gap
1 2 3 4 5 6 7 8 9 10	−	1 2 3 4 5 6 7 8 9 10	=	_____

Things I'm doing right: _____

_____

_____

_____

What goals can I set to improve in this area? _____

_____

_____

_____

Specific steps that I must take to achieve my improvement goals: _____

_____

_____

_____

_____

Action plan: _____

_____

_____

_____

_____

When I want to complete this: _____

_____

Proposals

When you've completed the bid, you must submit a written proposal that clarifies what your bid includes and what is not included. If your proposal is properly written and states the terms and conditions that you wish to have included, it's likely to be signed. At that point, you can consider the signed proposal a legal and binding contract.

Whenever you prepare a proposal, make sure it's delivered to the individual who is authorized to take action on it. Giving a proposal to a receptionist or secretary is a waste of time. If the prospect is sincerely interested in your company as a prospective contractor, they'll give you personal attention. Using others to deliver proposals may be taken as—well, we're not important! A proposal personally hand-delivered by the company owner implies the opposite. Perhaps the best salesman is the person who stands to gain the most—the company president.

Don't waste time on price shoppers. If you manage to get a job from them, you probably won't be able to make a reasonable profit, and you won't establish a permanent relationship because they'll dump you whenever someone underbids you.

Knowing what is said and what is not said in your major competitors' proposals and contracts can be used to your tactical advantage. Intelligence gathering and counter-intelligence is not limited to governments. Business is war! The more you know about the strengths and weaknesses of your opponent, the more likely you are to improve your own firm, and not lose money bidding against firms you can't beat. The performance of brand-X can be used as a benchmark for your own firm—somewhat like the time to beat!

A sample proposal is included in the back of this workbook. Proposals should be designed to protect you and the consumer. Take the time to design your proposal to achieve that purpose.

Related Topics:
- Contracts
- Legal

Proposals

Rate Importance	minus	My Skill Level	equals	Gap
1 2 3 4 5 6 7 8 9 10	−	1 2 3 4 5 6 7 8 9 10	=	_____

Things I'm doing right: _____

_____

_____

_____

What goals can I set to improve in this area? _____

_____

_____

_____

Specific steps that I must take to achieve my improvement goals: _____

_____

_____

_____

_____

Action plan: _____

_____

_____

_____

_____

When I want to complete this: _____

_____

Notes

Chapter

Labor Management (Employees)

The management, supervision, training, and care taking of employees are major factors in any business owner's or manager's day. In the final analysis, it's how well you and your employees perform that determines not only your profitability, but your survivability as well. Your employees are the foundation of your business and, with proper guidance, can be responsible for the success of the business. With consideration given to proper training and supervision at the onset, you can develop your staff in such a way that you can continue to operate proficiently, even at times when you're away from the office for extended periods of time. If your business cannot operate satisfactorily without you for two weeks, you've got plenty of work to do.

The test of a good manager is how he or she manages, motivates and relates with employees. How closely your company reaches its objectives depends largely on the efforts and accomplishments of your employees. You should recognize the desire of your employees to improve their position in life and increase their income. The more ambitious employee often has a goal to establish their own business, using the training with you to prepare them. Perhaps that's how you got your background training to start your own business. Although this is often a fear of management, statistics show that most individuals don't have the ambition, drive and expertise to start their own business.

If you value the services of an employee who shows interest in going off on his/her own, you may want to use their talents within your organization rather than watching them become a competitor. Give them some of the benefits they would derive as an owner by offering such incentives as a share of the profits, health insurance for their family, and bonuses. Show them how they're better off with increased income, prestige, recognition, community standing and respect without the financial problems and possibility of joining the large majority of new companies that don't get off the ground. Fear and discomfort of personal failure can make the present comfort and related success look much better.

If one or more of your customers leave with an employee starting out on his/her own, you're not doing a proper job with your customers. Many businesses in all fields start with an employee moving out and taking customers with them. Make sure you have a personal relationship with each of your customers. Don't vent your anger with employees who leave to start their own business. Leave the door open for them to return on a friendly basis. Call them after a reasonable period of time, and let them know they're still welcome in your organization. Never criticize former employees in front of anyone, particularly your current employees.

Know your employees as the individual human beings that they are. Find out what their goals are. Gain their respect by being fair and equitable to all. Establish a model of behavior by your own actions—its called leadership! Let them know that upgrading and promotions will be made from within whenever possible, and keep this promise. Evaluate your employees on a regular schedule, perhaps twice a year, and express appreciation for good results.

A note on moonlighting (for service organizations primarily)—accept it as part of the business because just about every field employee does it. But control it! Set the ground rules. No moonlighting for your customers. No using your tools and equipment (unless you're willing to loan them). No using your materials (unless you're willing to sell them). No using your trucks. Don't let the employee get away with unapproved use of your facilities. Ask them if they must moonlight to at least not wear their company uniforms. Ask that they build up their own reputations, not borrow from you and their fellow employees who have worked hard to build up too. Let employees know their limits and what cooperation they can expect from you.

The following guidelines will help you establish a good relationship with and promote quality work from your employees:

- **Don't assume your employees know what you want.** Explain what you want and provide training. Be sure they understand fully the task at the conclusion of training. Then have their supervisor follow-up to confirm that they are correctly applying the training they received.

- **Set deadlines.** Be realistic and maintain contact along the way to be sure that the schedule is being met.
- **Get an understanding about what will be done if work isn't satisfactory.** You have a right to get the quality of work that you expect and the employee should realize what the consequences will be if this standard is not met.
- **Treat the people you hire like adults.** Treat them with consideration, thoughtfulness and understanding. Greet your employees each day, compliment them for appearance or accomplishment and, most importantly, listen to them when they speak to you.
- **Pay on time.**
- **Reward good work** either with praise, bonus, or increased responsibility, if desired.

The following pages will detail some of the topics relating to Labor Management.

Chapter 4—Labor Management (Employees) Table of Contents

Appearance of Office

Office appearance is important to employees. A professional and neat working environment builds company morale and increases the proficiency of staff members. It also instills confidence in the visitors to the office as to your success and abilities. Most employees would like to point with pride to the firm where they work.

Individuals have different work styles and habits. There are many products on the market that are available to help someone sort, maintain, and keep their work materials filed and organized while maintaining a neat appearance. You must let your employees know what you consider to be acceptable standards for their working areas and allow them to operate within your standards.

An office policy, such as a clean desktop at the end of the day (while nice) has not been proven to be necessary. Not eating at your desk when a break-room is provided can be justified on the basis of rodent control. If you develop standard policies, make sure that they are fair and sensible. I recall a business owner who would never hire a person who smoked a pipe, as pipe smokers wasted too much time.

Provide sufficient files, furniture and equipment so that papers, catalogs, equipment, etc., can be stored safely and neatly. Establish procedures for the office to be cleaned on a regular basis, and for the grounds and parking areas to be cleaned and re-striped on a scheduled basis.

As a manager, you are a role model for your employees and you should be organized and neat. Set a standard for the organization, and enforce your standards consistently.

Appearance of Office

Rate Importance	minus	My Skill Level	equals	Gap
1 2 3 4 5 6 7 8 9 10	–	1 2 3 4 5 6 7 8 9 10	=	_____

Things I'm doing right: _____

_____

_____

_____

What goals can I set to improve in this area? _____

_____

_____

_____

Specific steps that I must take to achieve my improvement goals: _____

_____

_____

_____

_____

Action plan: _____

_____

_____

_____

_____

_____

When I want to complete this: _____

_____

Basic Needs

The four most basic needs of an individual are food, clothing, shelter, and freedom from fear. Most individuals begin a job in order to fill these four basic needs in their lives. With luck and careful selection of employees, you'll find that your employees will develop a fifth "need"— that is to grow to become an integral and confident part of your organization.

Allowing individuals to fill their most basic needs on the job and, at the same time, develop their personal skills and abilities to become more productive and proficient for your organization is important. Unacceptable behavior in the workplace must not be tolerated. Make sure that your firm has and enforces policies that do not tolerate negative behavior among employees.

When employees must work late to complete company business, make sure that they have someone check on them from time to time. Maintain outdoor lighting for access and egress to the work site. At night it is important when they leave the office late that they don't have to enter a dark parking lot.

Always remember to treat your employees with respect. Be available to listen to them, and acknowledge their presence and their accomplishments.

Related Topics:
• Company Policy

Basic Needs

Rate Importance	minus	My Skill Level	equals	Gap
1 2 3 4 5 6 7 8 9 10	–	1 2 3 4 5 6 7 8 9 10	=	_____

Things I'm doing right: _____

_____

_____

What goals can I set to improve in this area? _____

_____

_____

Specific steps that I must take to achieve my improvement goals: _____

_____

_____

_____

Action plan: _____

_____

_____

_____

_____

When I want to complete this: _____

_____

Company Policy

Every company should have a written policy and procedure for all tasks to be accomplished, as well as an Employee Handbook covering the rules of employment that all employees need to review at the time of their employment.

There are many ways to prepare an Employee Handbook, but most include the most basic information, such as starting and ending time, breaks, lunch, paid and unpaid holidays, vacations and eligibility, benefits and eligibility, pay periods, advances, use of company property for personal use, grounds for termination, etc. Policies should be established regarding infraction of rules and the possible consequences, including reasons for termination, written and oral warnings, etc.

A table of contents for a comprehensive (but not exhaustive) office policy manual could include the following topics:

Company Benefits:

- Medical Coverage
- Personal Days
- Sick Days
- Paid Holidays
- Vacation
- Bonus/Longevity Bonus
- Benefits in General
- Illness
- Late Arrival/Early Departure

Business Conduct:

- Business Conduct in General
- Social Media Policy
- Internet and Authorized Web Browsing
- Copy, Postage and UPS Services for Personal Use
- Equipment and Furniture
- Mailing Address
- Telephone Calls
- Visitors
- Letters of Recommendation
- Food and Drink on Premises

Court Appearance:

- Verification of Appearances
- Jury Duty
- Acting as a Witness

Daily Schedule:

- Lunch/Coffee Breaks
- Employee Production
- Timecards
- Paychecks
- Dress Code

Grounds for Immediate Dismissal:

- Drug/Substance Abuse
- Theft
- Discussion of Salaries
- Probationary Period
- Evaluations

Overtime:

- Fair Labor Law Act
- Exemptions
- Part-Time Employees

Performance Reviews.

Communication/Noncompliance:

- Dismissal Procedure

Hiring Policy:

- Hiring Agency Personnel
- Supervisors
- Relatives
- Loans

Miscellaneous:

- Radios/cell phones
- Ordering Supplies

- Answering Machine
- Air Conditioning
- Bathroom Supplies
- General Purchases

Employment Agreement:

This is recommended to be included. It would state that the employee has read and fully understands the contents of the manual and that they agree to comply with all safety policies and procedures.

Acknowledgment:

This is a basic statement indicating that the provisions included in the manual are subject to change and that revised copies will be distributed to all employees for review. It further states that receipt of the policy manual is not a contract for employment.

Noncompliance Forms:

These are forms designed to document written warnings for infractions of rules. Each company should have its own procedure established for hiring new employees, including commercially available application forms or those designed specifically for your organization.

You may wish to consider preparing a new employee checklist, which would document that the new employee has been properly introduced to co-workers, toured the new offices, understands and agrees with the contents of the policy manual, received training and other direction in his/her area of hire, etc. An employee termination and exit survey checklist can offer insights that you may not be aware of.

There are commercially available forms and workbooks that can help you organize your firm's policies better. You can purchase them at discount office supply stores or by catalog. It's often cost-effective to research these items and determine their necessity. Occasionally, your local library and the Internet can offer help in this task. In cards, nothing beats four aces; in business, nothing beats having it in writing!

Related Topics:
- Hiring & Firing

Company Policy

Rate Importance	minus	My Skill Level	equals	Gap
1 2 3 4 5 6 7 8 9 10	–	1 2 3 4 5 6 7 8 9 10	=	_____

Things I'm doing right: _____

_____

_____

_____

What goals can I set to improve in this area? _____

_____

_____

_____

Specific steps that I must take to achieve my improvement goals: _____

_____

_____

_____

_____

Action plan: _____

_____

_____

_____

_____

_____

When I want to complete this: _____

_____

Company Procedures

Your Policy and Procedure Manual can take many forms and will be shaped by the type of operation that you have. Just like your Employee Handbook covers guidelines for conditions of employment, this manual will cover guidelines for the company systems and processes, defined by the way YOU want your business to be run.

The Purpose. The importance of customer satisfaction and building your image and reputation cannot be overstated. You can achieve this by having a consistent way of operating your business so that your customer knows what to expect every time and your employees know what to deliver. Having a standard process that is written and always followed for every aspect of your business goes a long way to ensuring this . Once the process is defined and written, every employee knows what the expectation is and how to complete a task. If someone is away from the office because of an illness or a valued employee leaves to pursue other interests, your business can continue to function if the step-by-step procedure of what they do is recorded. If you have a person that processes your payroll on a weekly basis, the last thing that you want is for your employees not to get paid if that person can't perform the task for whatever reason. If the systems and procedures for payroll are in place, your employees get paid, no matter who processes payroll. Having solid written procedures will also allow management to take time off without fear that the business will come to a grinding halt in their absence.

The Goal. Have all the tasks documented and available to all employees for training and reference purposes. The manual should be comprehensive and cover every aspect of your business. Also understand that this manual is a moving target! As you get smarter with your business, and as new technology gets introduced, so your way of operating will change, and so your Procedure for doing business will change. Pages should get updated and replaced.

Creating a Manual if you don't already have one can be a daunting project. You will definitely need to work on it slowly and steadily so that it doesn't find its way to that stack of dreaded paperwork that you never look at. You might want to consider starting in the department that you feel is the most important to you and that you know the least about. Or you might want to take a segment of the business that you are most passionate about and wish that your employees could follow your lead and work the way you do. Or start with what keeps you up at night. Write it down on paper, and get it moving.

Work with your employees. Many of them have innovative and creative ideas and they just haven't been asked for their input. The idea here is to have their buy-in for how the business should operate so that everyone's goals are being met. Employees need to know what is expected of them, and they want to be able to do a good job and be rewarded for it. They need to feel like they are part of the team and a part of building and growing the business. Having a Procedure Manual is like having a Play Book for success.

The Content. A step-by-step procedure for each task should be accompanied by all the **forms and checklists** that relate to getting that part of the job done. It can be organized in whichever way works best for you and your employees. The following topics are some suggestions, but the list is far from all-inclusive.

Accounting

- Accounts Payable
- Accounts Receivable
- Cash Management
- Financial Reporting
- New Hire Checklist
- Payroll
- Reports
- Tax Reporting

Sales & Customer Service

- Follow up on sales calls [sample letters & emails]
- Follow up on service calls [content and frequency]
- Sales Leads
- Schedule of Client Meetings
- Follow up on completion of a job [checklist]

Project Management

- Bidding and bid checklist
- Changes and Change Orders
- Contract Checklist [specify the critical things to look for and include/exclude from contracts]
- Equipment [include Handling and Maintenance]
- Inventory; process and forms
- Job Selection & Scheduling [guidelines for your criteria]
- Labor Unit Manuals
- On-site job checklist [make sure all aspects of the job get completed and all tools and material finds it's way home]
- Proposals [forms and checklists]
- Purchasing Materials and Renting Equipment
- Supplies and Suppliers

Marketing and Advertising

- Checklist [all aspects that need to be in an ad or marketing piece]
- Logos and color schemes
- Publications
- Templates

Reimbursement

- Advances
- Disallowances and Overpayments
- Final Billing
- Reimbursement Requests
- Time Payment by Contractor

Facilities Management

- Air-conditioning
- Cleaning Services
- Emergency Procedures
- Equipment
- Plumbing

Your Company's Organizational Chart should be a part of the Manual. This gives all employees a clear understanding of their role and how it interfaces with other employees in the company.

- Who does what?
- Who is responsible for what?
- Who reports to whom?

A copy should be printed and put in a binder that is kept in a place where everyone has access. The date should be a part of the formatting of the footer so that as policies or procedures change or get updated, the pages in the book that get replaced with have a reference point. An electronic copy should be available on the computers, particularly if you have a shared drive, so that everyone is working from the most current version.

Related Topics:
- Company Policy
- Delegation
- Motivation
- Listening and Learning

Company Procedures

Rate Importance	minus	My Skill Level	equals	Gap
1 2 3 4 5 6 7 8 9 10	–	1 2 3 4 5 6 7 8 9 10	=	_____

Things I'm doing right: _____

_____

_____

_____

What goals can I set to improve in this area? _____

_____

_____

_____

Specific steps that I must take to achieve my improvement goals: _____

_____

_____

_____

_____

Action plan: _____

_____

_____

_____

_____

_____

When I want to complete this: _____

_____

Dress Code

Dress in a manner appropriate to your position in your company and to make a positive impression on the people with whom you interact. The casual wear you might adopt for the jobsite is not appropriate for conferences with customers, architects, bankers or business meetings. When attending association meetings, dress in a manner that represents success in your position as owner or manager.

Your dress, overall appearance and attitude will be the factors on which people base their first impression of you. You have only one chance to make a first impression—make it a good one!

Appearance also should apply to your employees. Good grooming, professional attire appropriate for their positions should be required. Management should dress in a manner that alerts visitors to their position—either a jacket and tie (if applicable) or a neat business shirt is appropriate at this level. Secretaries and other clerical staff should wear outfits that are suitable for office work. Many offices have a dress code that prohibits wearing blue jeans and tennis shoes, or other such casual styles of dress. Members of the shipping and receiving crews should also dress accordingly.

Some may consider an office dress code to be a bit prudish, such as the requirement of many U.S. presidents that no one enter the oval office without a coat and tie on. Respect is earned in many ways—one step at a time.

Remember, appearance is the first thing noticed by customers or visitors to your office. It is important that all employees, especially those in the reception area, dress professionally and present a good overall appearance.

Dress Code

Rate Importance	minus	My Skill Level	equals	Gap
1 2 3 4 5 6 7 8 9 10	–	1 2 3 4 5 6 7 8 9 10	=	_____

Things I'm doing right: _____

_____

_____

_____

What goals can I set to improve in this area? _____

_____

_____

_____

Specific steps that I must take to achieve my improvement goals: _____

_____

_____

_____

_____

Action plan: _____

_____

_____

_____

_____

_____

When I want to complete this: _____

_____

Forms

Every business should have standard forms that are to be used for various office and business procedures. Such forms include those used to record incoming telephone calls, sales leads, proposals, and completed contracts. There are even forms that can be used for problem solving and flow charts.

Maintain completed forms on file for future reference and to expedite follow-up procedures. Create a checklist to ensure that all the key elements of the task are not forgotten.

Be sure that all employees use all forms consistently. Provide training and sample completed forms for everyone to review and learn the procedure for. Make note when an individual does not comply with your request in order to reinforce their use of the required forms.

Be sure that all forms are completed accurately. This will provide a written documentation of the all-important phases of your business and will provide consistency and confidence in your operation. Maintaining a central file of all forms used by your business helps in form control (keeping the proper number sequence) and reordering when necessary.

There are commercially available forms and workbooks that can help you organize your firm's procedure better. You can purchase them at discount office supply stores or by catalog. It's often cost-effective to research these items and determine their necessity. Occasionally, your local library and the Internet can offer help in this task.

Related Topics:
- Record Keeping
- Company Policy
- Company Procedures

Forms

Rate Importance	minus	My Skill Level	equals	Gap
1 2 3 4 5 6 7 8 9 10	–	1 2 3 4 5 6 7 8 9 10	=	_____

Things I'm doing right: _____

_____

_____

What goals can I set to improve in this area? _____

_____

_____

Specific steps that I must take to achieve my improvement goals: _____

_____

_____

_____

Action plan: _____

_____

_____

_____

_____

When I want to complete this: _____

_____

Hiring and Firing

There are four main situations that will indicate when you need to hire an employee or additional employees:

- When you don't have the skills and expertise to do a job
- When it will cost you more to do the job yourself than to hire someone else to do it
- When one person can't do the job
- When you hate doing a task that must be done

You must then determine if the person you need will be needed to work on a full-time or part-time basis as an employee or as an independent contractor. A written job description provides a clear description of the skills and abilities required to effectively complete the job you need done. Before you begin the interview process, it's best to have a job description designed as well as a basic compensation package developed for the prospective employee.

Make sure that you are familiar with the Labor and Employment laws, both at the federal level and in your state as they relate to wages, benefits, probation, termination, etc. The following are solid guidelines, but Labor Law prevails.

Finding the right people for your organization is usually a matter of looking carefully at past experience and present capabilities. Getting referrals from a previous employer or acquaintance is probably the best way. When that isn't possible, get and check references, look at samples of past work or track record, or provide a pre-employment test to determine actual skill level. Don't be surprised when previous employers will do little more than confirm employment dates. They may be doing so only as a matter of company policy to reduce the potential for lawsuits. What is your policy about providing referrals? You do have one, don't you?

During the interview process, raise the problems and concerns you have in relation to the work you are hiring for. If you are under a tight deadline or the workday is pressure filled, express your concern that the job can be done right and on time. Explain any special circumstances that the individual may be involved in, such as regular overtime, weekend work, fieldwork, driving to and from jobsites, etc. Then listen and watch the person respond. Do they appear to have solutions? Are they confident about handling the situations you present?

The success of your organization is largely based on the work performance of the employees you hire. Why hire someone you may eventually fire? What a waste of your time in interviewing, training, trying to solve their problems and making them adapt to company policies if you're not convinced from the beginning that this is the kind of employee you want in order to build a successful organization. When selecting an employee, make sure they understand the kind of performance you expect from them. Feel confident and be sure to check their references.

Establish a company policy that new employees are to be evaluated over a probation period before regular employment is offered. Print this policy on an application form and explain it to the applicant so that no doubt exists. Have a written contract outlining mutual responsibilities and obligations.

If a valued employee wants to terminate on his/her own volition, find out why. Should your efforts to keep them be unsuccessful, leave the door open for them to return at a later date under amicable conditions. Phone them after a period of several months to tell them how much their work was appreciated, and invite them to return. They may have decided they were better off with you as an employer, but were reluctant to make the first call.

But the time does come when you find the attitude or production of an employee is below your acceptable standards. Have the employee in for an interview held in confidentiality and privacy (it's a good idea to have a quiet observer to these interviews), giving enough time and limiting outside interruptions. Tell them what you like about them and specify where their performance is satisfactory. Try to find out the source of their problem and offer your help. Opening the lines of communication may uncover a situation or personal or work problems that can be resolved.

If there is no alternative to firing, do so without animosity. If there is a temporary problem that can be worked out, decide whether the employee is valuable enough for you to exercise patience. If you keep an employee, follow up with periodic checkups. Don't retain an employee who is unwilling to compromise or who sets a poor example for other employees within the organization. A firing is an admission by both parties that one or the other, or both, failed to prevent the termination.

Points to consider when hiring:

- Consider employees' potential for upgrade to positions of greater performance.
- Realistically consider the high cost of turnover in personnel.
- Develop a list of questions for applicants that provide the information you need to make a qualified employment decision.
- Determine the actual reason why an applicant left a former position.
- Check on references and verify past experience listed.
- Identify his/her short-range and long-range personal and professional objectives.

Points to consider when firing:

- Conduct corrective interviews.
- Determine if there is an ability problem or an attitude problem.
- Have a personal interview and prepare a written report signed by either management or the supervisor, and the employee. Date the report and maintain a copy in the personnel folder.
- Correct poor communication.
- You have a right to know what your employees are doing.
- Employees have a right to know what the consequences of their actions are.

Remember that ability problems can be solved. Attitude problems are more difficult to deal with.

Related Topics:
- Leadership
- Company Policy
- Job Descriptions and Responsibility

Hiring and Firing

Rate Importance	minus	My Skill Level	equals	Gap
1 2 3 4 5 6 7 8 9 10	−	1 2 3 4 5 6 7 8 9 10	=	_____

Things I'm doing right: _____

_____

_____

What goals can I set to improve in this area? _____

_____

_____

Specific steps that I must take to achieve my improvement goals: _____

_____

_____

_____

Action plan: _____

_____

_____

_____

_____

When I want to complete this: _____

_____

Job Descriptions and Responsibility

Establish a system in your office where each employee knows their responsibilities, and each function is handled in a timely and efficient manner. This is best accomplished by the design of a job description, including a priority listing of tasks.

A written job description provides a clear description of the skills and abilities required to effectively complete the job you need done. The description should be written for the position and work to be performed—not to accommodate someone who may currently be filling the position. The more objective the standards, the more effective you can be in matching performance and skills to the job.

Include on the job description form a space for providing training as well as who the training is to be provided by, and the date and acknowledgment by the employee that the training was provided and understood. This can eliminate many problems in the future.

The manager should not let himself get bogged down with office details, such as maintaining records, billing and collecting, correspondence and filing. Incoming phone calls should be screened, and unless the manager's personal attention is required, calls should be handled with information taken and given by someone else.

The following information can be used as a guideline for designing job descriptions. Be sure to include the title of the person (or job) that you are describing. List tasks in order of importance and assign priorities to these tasks. Indicate whether they should be accomplished on a daily, weekly or monthly basis, etc.

Obviously, you'll modify the list to suit the needs of your individual organization. Have others review the job description. You may find that other aspects of the job have migrated into the position without a lot of thought as to who should actually be completing these tasks.

1. Manager:

- Determine staffing requirements.
- Hire and train new staff.
- Set employee goals and objectives.
- Schedule projects in steps and budget time required to meet deadlines.
- Determine labor requirements for projects.
- Review projects to monitor compliance with building and safe codes and other regulations.
- Develop and implement productivity and quality control programs.
- Prepare contracts and negotiates revisions and changes.
- Allocate use of available resources.
- Evaluate current business processes and systems.
- Plan and implement procedures and systems to maximize operating efficiency.
- Purchase and manage insurance plans.

- Establish and maintain controls.
- Formulate policies and practices.
- Develop and implement marketing and sales plan.
- Coordinate financial and budget activities.
- Investigate damage, accidents or delays at project sites.
- Evaluate construction methods and determine cost-effectiveness of plans.

2. Estimator:

- Organize job plan.
- Make take-offs.
- List items for pricing.
- Develop job budget.
- Qualifications to consider: experience in trade; ability to work with detail; ability to follow procedure; ability to constantly work toward deadline under pressure.
- Estimate all jobs.
- Prepare bill of materials.
- Prepare all change orders.
- Visit jobsites.
- Consult with Purchasing Agent.
- Review plans for alternate methods.

3. Purchasing Agent:

- Order materials based on estimate, or from orders phoned in from the field.
- Check material received against purchase orders, including stock numbers.
- Check quantity and price.
- Check invoices—extensions, prices, and applicable discounts.
- Maintain a file on current prices.
- Schedule drivers for material pickup, tool transfers, etc.
- Maintain tool inventory.
- Maintain file on temporary poles.
- Order rental shacks and other equipment.
- Keep a maintenance log of trucks and cars.
- Maintain inventory in the warehouse and job trailers.

4. Receptionist/Secretary:

- Answer phones.
- Open mail.
- Greet people.
- Label folders and maintain files.
- Type correspondence, billing, etc.
- Type proposals and contracts.

- Handle outgoing mail.
- Receive and sign for packages.
- Keep office presentable.
- Check office inventory and replace when necessary.

5. Bookkeeper:

- Payroll
- Accounts Payable
- Accounts Receivable
- General ledger
- Government reports
- Current records
- Late payment statements
- Job cost evaluations

6. Superintendent:

- Organizes, coordinates and supervises the work of the Foreman, Sub and employees on construction projects.
- Interviews, hires and trains employees.
- Determines work priorities and coordinates work activities.
- Coordinates new construction and major remodeling.
- Schedules meetings and reviews project documents as necessary.
- Collaborates with administrators on supervision of all work.
- Keeps cost records on work performed and materials.
- Responsible for control of costs in materials and wages.
- Schedules jobs and operations.
- Controls construction progress in order to complete within time limits.
- Estimates materials needed including manpower.
- Inspects day to day construction work to enforce conformity to specifications.
- Promotes job site safety and rectifies job site hazards immediately.
- Maintains an organized job site, including the construction office.
- Other related duties as assigned.

Related Topics:
- Company Policy
- Company Procedures
- Hiring and Firing

Job Descriptions and Responsibility

Rate Importance	minus	My Skill Level	equals	Gap
1 2 3 4 5 6 7 8 9 10	−	1 2 3 4 5 6 7 8 9 10	=	_____

Things I'm doing right: _____

_____

_____

_____

What goals can I set to improve in this area? _____

_____

_____

_____

Specific steps that I must take to achieve my improvement goals: _____

_____

_____

_____

_____

Action plan: _____

_____

_____

_____

_____

When I want to complete this: _____

_____

Meetings

Meetings should serve to accomplish a specific goal. Before scheduling a meeting, ask yourself if the matter could be handled by phone or by mail. To keep meetings efficient, limit their length. If you don't complete your agenda within the allotted time, you can schedule another meeting or follow up by phone or mail. Time limits force people to say what they have to say and hear what they have to hear quickly, with fewer diversions into nonessential details.

The purpose of your key employee meetings is not to complain about problems or assign blame, but to find solutions. Meetings are more productive as a means of exchanging ideas rather than announcing statements of policy. You want a dialogue, not a lecture.

Meetings should be held on a scheduled basis, with ample advance notice, at a time that suits the majority of the participants. Circulate an agenda and inform the participants in advance the topics of discussion. It's important that meetings have written agendas; those that do not are too easily misdirected.

If you hold them before the day's work starts, have breakfast served. If at the end of the workday, have a snack brought in. Have a structured agenda prepared in advance. Keep it interesting and try to have everyone present participate instead of it being dominated by one or two people. Foremen or supervisors should schedule meetings with their crews. Give everyone the opportunity to contribute to the company's welfare.

Common problems involved with meetings include:

- Wrong time of day or week
- No advance notice
- Meetings focus on problems and blame assignment and not solutions
- A meeting is scheduled, but it becomes a lecture
- No planned agenda
- Manager lacks conference leadership
- No summary at conclusion of meeting, no assignment of action tasks, and no follow-up
- A few people do all the talking—counsel them privately to allow or better help others to contribute. It's just a matter of showing respect for others
- Decision-makers are not at the meeting

There are some people that will not comment or offer any input in a meeting. Some people are private and prefer not to express their feelings. See if that person can work on a project for you and provide you with feedback. Don't give a negative evaluation because of this.

Learn to use body language to signal the end of a meeting or appointment. Shut your notebook, pick up your papers, rise and begin moving toward the door, using closing comments like "I'm glad we could meet," "we got a lot done," or "I'll look forward to hearing from you soon."

Related Topics:
• Leadership

Meetings

Rate Importance	minus	My Skill Level	equals	Gap
1 2 3 4 5 6 7 8 9 10	–	1 2 3 4 5 6 7 8 9 10	=	_____

Things I'm doing right: _____

_____

_____

_____

What goals can I set to improve in this area? _____

_____

_____

_____

Specific steps that I must take to achieve my improvement goals: _____

_____

_____

_____

_____

Action plan: _____

_____

_____

_____

_____

When I want to complete this: _____

_____

Peter Principle

NOTE: The Peter Principle concept was introduced by Canadian sociologist Dr. Laurence Johnston Peter in his humoristic book of the same title. In his book, he describes the pitfalls of the bureaucratic organization witnessed during his extensive research into business organizations. This book is available online and in some bookstores.

This principle describes the practice of promoting employees until they reach a position at the threshold of their incompetence. Avoid this by training employees for the job before advancing them. Make sure they qualify. Why transfer them from a position where they were doing a good job into one they can't handle. Competence in doing one kind of job does not guarantee the same level of competence in a more demanding position.

The problem is not with the promotion, but rather with the lack of education and training to prepare for the new duties. Make it possible for your employees to learn their trade or enhance their skills so that they can first increase their productivity, and then qualify for advancement.

The affected individuals can also cause this problem. Some people are unwilling to give up responsibility to someone else. They maintain a feeling that no one can complete a task as efficiently as they can. On occasion, some individuals will attempt to take on additional responsibility without relinquishing a portion of their past responsibilities and find themselves in a highly stressful situation. Although they can perform all tasks effectively in theory, it proves to be impossible in actual practice.

Let your employees know that you will distribute responsibility based on performance, experience and need in specific areas. To relinquish former responsibility should not be looked on as a threat, but rather a positive change to increase one's proficiency in a needed area. Stressing the need for people to be flexible so that the organization can be flexible helps to make changes seem less negatively stressful.

Peter Principle

Rate Importance	minus	My Skill Level	equals	Gap
1 2 3 4 5 6 7 8 9 10	−	1 2 3 4 5 6 7 8 9 10	=	_____

Things I'm doing right: _____

_____

_____

_____

What goals can I set to improve in this area? _____

_____

_____

_____

Specific steps that I must take to achieve my improvement goals: _____

_____

_____

_____

_____

Action plan: _____

_____

_____

_____

_____

When I want to complete this: _____

_____

Salary

The impact of competitiveness between contractors because of the difference in pay scale can be significant. Some contractors pay rock bottom salaries and others pay above union scale. Pay top dollar and get highly skilled, motivated, educated and trained employees. The result will be an increase in labor productivity.

If you pay a low salary, your better employees will leave to do the same work somewhere else or go to work on their own. Only the poorer, less motivated and less able employees will remain to work for you for lower pay. In addition, you may expect code violations, increased supervision requirements, and an increase in lower productivity.

To expand your work force, make an effort to hire quality people, pay them accordingly, and provide them with proper training. Make it possible for them to learn their trade or enhance their skills so that they can first increase their productivity, and then qualify for advancement. Many of today's successful contractors have an apprenticeship and continuing training program for their employees.

Overpaying, however, has a drawback also. You can be less competitive in the price you charge for the product or the service that you are offering. In business, every dollar spent must produce a positive return and that includes dollars invested in wages and salaries.

Compensation consists of more than salary (dollars):

- **Working Environment.** Providing a clean, safe and professional working environment encourages employees to act with higher proficiency and professionalism. It also serves to instill pride in their accomplishments and makes them happy to come to work.
- **Terms of Employment.** Some employees may request and have a legitimate need for different working hours per day, per week, etc. Weigh your needs against those of your employees and determine if the work you need can be completed on these terms. By providing favorable terms of employment, you are instilling pride and purpose to your employees. Exercise care to treat everyone equally. Should you grant a new hire a benefit you denied existing employees, you may have created problems for not only the new hire (resentment by others) but yourself as well with existing employees who may have been denied the same benefit in the past.
- **Status.** Added responsibility and accountability, as well as a title, often serve to provide immeasurable pride to an employee who is qualified and earns the status.
- **Fringe Benefits.** These could include insurance coverage for the employee and family, company car or vehicle, uniforms, profit sharing, stock if applicable, increased vacation days, association membership, and training classes, to name but a few. Dollars invested in an employee break-room don't have to be matched with payment

of social security and unemployment taxes. Some benefits are taxable, while others are not. Some benefit only one employee, others several employees. Be creative!

- **Benefits.** These include insurance for the employee, paid holidays, and scheduled vacations. The daily newspaper, professional association dues, company paid defensive driving, and health club memberships offer a menu for employees to choose from. Again, be creative!

Related Topics:
- Company Policy
- Hiring & Firing

Salary

Rate Importance	minus	My Skill Level	equals	Gap
1 2 3 4 5 6 7 8 9 10	–	1 2 3 4 5 6 7 8 9 10	=	_____

Things I'm doing right: _____

_____

_____

_____

What goals can I set to improve in this area? _____

_____

_____

_____

Specific steps that I must take to achieve my improvement goals: _____

_____

_____

_____

_____

Action plan: _____

_____

_____

_____

_____

When I want to complete this: _____

Annex

Action Plan

By now you have an idea of all the aspects that are involved in running a successful business, and if you've completed the skills worksheets along with every section you know the areas that you need to focus on improving. But it is still a daunting task. What do you do next?

Having a Business Model is essential; it defines how your company creates, delivers and captures value, and is an integral part of all your decision-making and business strategy. If you're just beginning, you probably need direction on how to get started. If you've been in business for years, this is probably a good time to review your company's business model and see if there are guidelines or standards that have run their course and should be updated. Whether you are a one-man shop or have many employees, having your business philosophy and standards in writing is crucial. Not only will this free up your time, but because all the major decisions have been made, it will reduce your stress levels and can only result in you being more productive and profitable.

This Annex contains some Business Model action guidelines and example forms appropriate for your needs. Here's what we are including for you:

- **Business Model.** Mike has created an invaluable tool to help you build your business model. This series of Action Guidelines illustrates the kinds of decisions you need to make to establish what your own business goals are, who your customers are, what they want, and how you can best meet their needs, get paid for doing so, and make a profit.
- **Business Development Worksheet.** This worksheet will help you keep track of all the items in your business model.
- **Daily Log Example.**
- **Organizational Chart Example.**
- **Customer Survey Example.**
- **Employee Survey Example.**
- **Proposal for Electrical Work Examples.**

Other Resources: The following books are just a few of many that will give you a new and different perspective on personal achievement as well as moving your life and your business forward.

- *The Slight Edge* (Revised Edition): *Turning Simple Disciplines Into Massive Success*, by Jeff Olson.
- *The E-Myth Revisited: Why Most Small Businesses Don't Work and What to Do About It*, by Michael E. Gerber.
- *Eat That Frog!: 21 Great Ways to Stop Procrastinating and Get More Done in Less Time*, by Brian Tracy.

Business Model

O nly you (and your team) can decide what standards, principles and practices best represent your business. The example below is for an Emergency Service Electrical Contractor, providing services directly for the owner of the property, or for the property manager – 24/7/365. The Action steps outlined are appropriate for that type of business. We're providing them to you as a guideline, and you can use them as a starting point, or create your own action steps based on your individual needs and business type.

Business Model Action Guidelines—Company XYZ

The goal of this business is to make as much money as possible with the least amount of effort to provide life-long employment for our employees. Employees are to receive a reasonable salary, benefits, and bonuses. In addition, the business model is designed to provide the owner with personal financial security

Accounting System

Our accounting system must be constructed to provide not only tax and mandated data, but financial management data as well. Among the records to be maintained are time cards, proposals, estimates, job-costing, analyses, contracts, permits, tax records, payroll records, inventory, tool locations, and truck costs.

Actions

Action 1:   If we say we will do something, we do it—no excuses.

Action 2:   Respect those that are doing something for us at no charge.

Action 3:   Be honest.

Action 4:   Don't be condescending.

Action 5:   Over deliver (be on time).

Action 6:   In order to get ahead, we have to do the right thing; then we have to do the right thing, and then we have to do the right thing.

Aging Report

It's critical that all accounts receivable be paid timely and none are to exceed 30 days.

Action 1:   Set a schedule for running the aging report—every time we invoice? Once a week?

Action 2:   Invoice on Time!

Action 3:   Finance to produce an aging report monthly and all past due accounts must be paid.

Action 4:   Any accounts 60 days are to be handled by the finance department; choose the strongest person to handle collections.

Action 5:   Accounts 90 days are to be sent to a collection person.

Bad Checks

Generally the reason for a bad check is the improper selection of the customer.

Action 1:   Finance department to collect the money; the owner to remain the "good guy."

Banking/Banker

Action 1:   Have a small community bank; [when we walk in the door they know us. We can call up and get better, quicker action].

Action 2:   Get a line of credit; it will help us to get our line of credit if we can get our vendors to write a letter that says we pay our bills on time.

Action 3: Embezzlement! Pay attention. Have the bank statement sent to a special PO Box, not the office, and always review it. Usually the person stealing from you is indispensable; they do everything for you, they take care of your calendar, your family gifts, your payments, and your whole business. They work hard, they stay late, they're always there, and they have access to your checkbook [and all your other information]. They know exactly what's going on in the business and if they were inclined to do so, they have easy access to steal from you.

Action 4: The person who writes the checks cannot be the one to balance our checkbook.

Action 5: Never sign a check unless we have the original invoice attached to it. Initial the original invoice.

Barter

Bartering is not of any value unless the value received is two times the exchange services. It is typically more cost effective to get paid for work performed.

Action 1: No barter agreements unless approved by the Finance Manager in advance.

Action 2: Policy is to only approve barter when the customer has no money and we want something.

Bids

Action 1: Bid only jobs where we have the technical, financial, and manpower capabilities, where the job can be visited daily at a profit margin established by Finance.

Action 2: We do not bid with contractors, unless approved by Finance.

Action 3: We do not bid or associate with anybody that gives us a bad feeling in our gut, such as those that want a discount, are pushy, disrespectful, or want to provide the material.

Action 4: Maximum bid dollar value is $25,000 unless otherwise approved by Finance.

Action 5: Only bid jobs that are within 1 hour of house as established by GPS unless approved by Finance.

Action 6: Bids to include material supplied by us; customer typically supplies lighting fixtures.

Action 7: Permit fee not to be included in the bid price, but to be shown as a separate line item. The labor to secure permit fee is included in overhead.

Action 8: For larger bids have someone review the bid, then put together the proposal for owner's review, approve and send to the customer, and get them a price in 48 hours.

Action 9: Software: If we don't bid contract work it doesn't justify software; if this model was not a service contractor business, and was to bid lots of jobs, then we would need to consider it.

Action 10: We don't bid on a job that we know for a fact we won't get. Be strong enough to stay "NO", and recommend the customer to an estimating service, or charge them a fee for the bid.

Bids—Slow

Verbal—No charge
Travel within 30 minutes—No charge
Travel within 45 minutes—No charge
Travel within 1 hour—No charge

Bids—Normal Work Load

Verbal—No charge
Travel within 30 minutes—$10, credited with job
Travel within 45 minutes—$20, credited with job
Travel within 1 hour—$30, credited with job

Bids—Busy

Verbal—No charge
Travel within 30 minutes—$20, credited with job
Travel within 45 minutes—$30, credited with job
Travel within 1 hour—$50, credited with job

Bills

Action 1:   All bills to be paid when due.

Action 2:   Where option to pay in full results in savings, then this option is to always be taken.

Bonus

Bonus is something we want to always provide where finance permits; we will try to give bonuses as follows based on the past five years of sales:

Record month sales—One week pay
2nd best month sales—Three days' pay
3rd best month sales—One day pay

Record quarter sales—One week pay
2nd best quarter sales—Three days' pay
3rd best quarter sales—One day pay

Record year sales—One week pay
2nd best year sales—Three days' pay
3rd best year sales—One day pay

Business Expenses versus Personal

Action 1:   Establish separate financial records and credit cards for personal and business expenses and do not mix the two.

Action 2:   Establish rules about what qualifies as a business expense. Do not use the business account as a personal bank.

Busy Times

Busy Times can create more problems than if times are slow.

Action 1:   When times are busy we will find a way to be very conservative, and put money away for the hard times; pay for equipment, put money in the bank;

Action 2:   We will stay with our business plan, draw and expense budget; at the end of the year, take any "bonus" earned.

Action 3:   We won't lose track of running the business by working "in" the business (worker-bee) instead of "on" the business.

Action 4:   We will never make money if we're stressed; it becomes unmanageable.

Change Orders

It's critical to maintain communication on pricing at all times.

Action 1:   Change order pricing must be submitted to the customer via email with a request for approval within 24 hours of the request.

Action 2:   Change orders are to be priced in accordance with the pricing model that was used to create the bid; this includes credits.

Action 3:   We establish a standard (boiler-plate) change-order process and review it in advance with the customer so we don't have to negotiate it after the job. If a change order is made and it wasn't priced or agreed to in advance and there is a disagreement, the customer is right, and we shouldn't expect to be paid. A lot of this has to do with the relationship between us and the customer.

Action 4:   In the event that there is no signed change order, and it is in the middle of the job, every change order needs to be acknowledged as it is being done; we keep a list of everything that is done, get a price for each one, and send the invoice immediately.

Codes & Standards

It is absolutely imperative to stay current in the electrical code. Hard to stay current while you're running an operation so make sure that we sign up for an annual class and commit to being there.

Communications

Action 1:   Out of respect for others, all emails, phone calls, or text messages are to be responded to immediately, Monday—Friday; this does not mean that we have to take care of the request, but we must acknowledge it.

Action 2:   For jobs that take more than one day, the customer is to be updated at all times on the progress of the job. A list of items should be updated and sent to the customer to include its status: completed, pending and reason, such as other trades, material, etc. In addition the email should also include when we will be at the job and when each item is to be completed.

Action 3:   All completion dates/times must be done in advance; better to under-promise and over-deliver.

Action 4:   We communicate effectively with the people on our staff, especially those out in the field.

Action 5:   We have an established sequence of communication with customer so we don't waste time; email to confirm appointment, phone call day before; another phone call before we leave for the job.

Continued Education

Success Programs are essential to keep motivated and get new ideas; classes and seminars are a must in order to keep up with the Code and stay current.

Action 1:   We have a calendar of continuing education classes and seminars, and schedule the people and the time at the beginning of the year, and stick to the schedule.

Action 2:   I will institute a training program so that there are competent people to run the business. I need to rearrange my life so that I don't need to be present!

Continuous Improvement

Success is not a destination—it is part of the journey. It takes time to accumulate wealth.

Action 1:   We READ constantly (10 pages a day)

Action 2:   Everything we do should be better the next time.

Action 3:   We don't spend more than we make. We don't buy something unless we have the cash to buy it—never make payments in order to "acquire" something [a house being the exception and take a 15 year mortgage].

Contract Conditions

Since we are an emergency electrical service contractor, we generally have no reason to sign a customer contract.

Action 1:   No contracts to be signed unless approved by Finance.

Action 2:   We will provide our terms and conditions with all bids via Fresh Books.

Action 3:   We never submit a proposal that we have pre-signed. It becomes a contract upon their signature. If we don't sign it we have an opportunity to re-negotiate it, or not accept it if our conditions have changed or if we decide we don't want to do the job.

Contract Work—Owner

There are no special requirements associated with working directly with the owner, other than ensuring the proper customer type.

Contractor Work—General Contractor

Because general contractors are used to beating up their subs, it's our policy to not perform any work for general contractors. However, if an opportunity arises we will consider GC work under the following conditions:

Action 1:   Finance department must give approval after a thorough investigation into the contractor. The following information is required: business name, owner name, GC License #, two vendors, three subs, and copy of contract.

Action 2:   Contractor must comply with customer type requirements.

Credit Card Usage

Action 1:   Only use a credit card to spend more money than we make if we're making an investment in something that is going to make us more money and benefit the business in the long run.

Action 2:   We have a personal credit card and a business credit card, and use them appropriately. We ALWAYS pay the balance at the end of the month.

Crusades

We will not take up a crusade until we are established and our business is running well, and we have the time and energy for it.

Customer Type/Selection

The right customer for our organization is critical for our success. This ensures reduced bad debt, less stress, and improved efficiency and work quality.

Action 1:   The customer must have an electrical service need (problem).

Action 2:   The customer must have the funds to pay for the service at the time the service is provided.

Action 3:   The customer must be authorized to make the decision/payment.

Action 4:   The customer must value our service and appreciate our efforts.

Action 5:   No work to be performed for general contractors, unless approved by the Finance Dept.

Action 6:   Caution on performing work for those that want a "discount", "senior discount", "coupon".

Daily Log

Action 1:   Rate ourselves daily on how we think we did for the day. For example:

- Job management skills
- Electrical installation performance
- What time did we start administrative work? Etc.
- What positive thoughts did we have today?

Action 2:   If we constantly work around something to get it done then there must be a solution—make a change/purchase, etc.

Action 3:   Take a look every day to see what we can do to make it better and more efficient the next time.

Discounts

Action 1:   All payments made by check are at the agreed price, no discount.

Action 2:   If the customer requests a discount for cash payment, give the customer 3% off the entire bill.

Action 3:   If the customer requests payment via credit card, there is an additional charge of 3%. This is our business model: do a proper evaluation. If we are going to take credit cards, we need to understand that it will cost us 3% in fees—we might need to change our pricing structure to accommodate this practice.

Draw

The purpose of the business is to make the owner the most amount of money with the least amount of effort. The owner is entitled to a "draw" at the end of the year based on the following:

Action 1:   0% of profit—if less than one month of average sales is in the business money market account

Action 2:   20% of profit—if between one and two months of average sales is in the business money market account

Action 3:   30% of profit—if between two and three months of average sales is in the business money market account

Action 4:   40% of profit—if between three and four months of average sales is in the business money market account

Action 5:   50% of profit—if between four and five months of average sales is in the business money market account

Action 6:   60% of profit—if between five and six months of average sales is in the business money market account

Action 7:   70% of profit—if more than six months of average sales is in the business money market account.

Note: "Monthly average sales" is determined by taking the annual sales divided by 12 months.

Dress Code

Action 1:   The owner must at all times be as professional as possible. When working on the job, "job dress code" is acceptable. When visiting the customer, the owner needs when possible to dress "for the customer". Any time the owner is out at a seminar or other professional function white shirt and tie is the minimum.

Action 2:   Job dress code involves long pants and company polo shirts; however when "dirt" work is involved, the dress code is permitted to be shorts and Company t-shirt (short or long sleeve).

Action 3:   Company is to provide all employees with five polo and five t-shirts.

Action 4:   Bare chest is never permitted on the job site.

Employee Relations

The goal is to have life-long employees that value an honest company.

Action 1:   These employees are to be treated with honor and respect.

Action 2:   The employees are to receive a fair salary with full benefits and bonuses when possible.

Action 3:   We hire those with the best driving record, credit, no criminal record, and non-smoker.

Action 4:   We will remove immediately any employee that is not a team member.

Action 5:   Employees are only hired when overtime is excessive and there is a long term need.

Action 6:   Employee benefits can be reduced to maintain profit margins.

Action 7:   Employee salary can be reduced to maintain profit margins.

Action 8:   Employee hours can be reduced to maintain profit margins.

Action 9:   Electricians are not to be paid standard rates for nontechnical hours.

Equipment

To ensure efficient operation of the company in all areas, 100% of everything mechanical and electronic must be in perfect operation, both personal and business.

Action 1:   Vehicles must be serviced on time and all concerns fixed immediately.

Action 2:   All tools must be serviced and purchased so that they are always available.

Action 3:   Office equipment must be operational without any glitches.

Action 4:   We do not buy new equipment if we are thinking about getting into a new area of work. Wait until we know we have been doing that work for a while, will continue to do it, and really need to buy it instead of continuing to rent it—and pay cash for it if we buy it!

Estimating Systems

Even though manual estimates are good for very small projects (especially if we use unit pricing) this method is not efficient for the electrical contractor who is regularly bidding jobs.

Action 1:   Analyze the business; are we too big? What kind of work do we do? Do we have someone who's an expert at spreadsheets? This will determine whether we can create our own estimating tool or whether we need to subscribe to a service, or buy a system.

Family

Action 1:   God has blessed us with a special gift; we should take that gift to bless others at no charge, except the cost of material.

Action 2:   Commercial property service—Our choice to do work, but the fee is our standard rate.

Finance

Proper financial management is key to meeting the company's business model.

Action 1:   Have a Financial Manager that understands good construction business finance practices.

Action 2:   Have a financial plan as follows.

- Transfer 5% of all sales to business savings account.
- Transfer 5% of all sales to personal savings account until the balance equals six months of owner salary.
- Pay the owner no more than a journeyman electrician.
- Loan Balance—At the end of the month, any monies over $15,000 in checking are to be transferred to pay off any loans outstanding. If there is no loan, that extra goes to money market fund.

Action 3:   Owner is not to "borrow" any money from the business.

Action 4:   Owner is not permitted to run personal expenses through the business.

Action 5:   Owner is permitted to use up to 5% of business income for owner incidental expenses.

Forecasting

Action 1:   Downsizing. We commit to watch the trends carefully, and have a plan for what to do when things crash. We have to make money on every job; we have to make money every week, every month, every year. If we don't make money we know immediately. Why? Analyze it. We can't lose money. Work "on" the business. Be aware.

Action 2:   Scaling Down: We will not wait till we run out of money and then have to get rid of everyone. We do the critical thinking. Slowly implement cutbacks and scale back to get where we need to be to save the business and keep it running. If we don't have cash flow, sit down with our banker and make an investment.

Action 3:   Growth when the economy changes—we need to know how far we can go, and how to do it successfully so we can grow slowly and always make money (not get intoxicated by the success as we go). Make a plan so our business must always be manageable. When we're getting more calls and are too busy, we will raise our prices and increase our profit margins. We can become more selective of the customer and the type of work so that we can make more profit with fewer jobs.

Friends

Action 1:   Charge the standard rate and give them standard service unless we feel we want to give them a discount [of no more than 50%], but the service can only be completed when we are slow, nights, or weekends.

Action 2:   Protect friends and family relationships [sometimes hard to do business with them]. If we work closely with another company, we should consider referring friends to him or her: "Call xxx, tell him you're my friend, he'll take care of you."

Action 3:   We NEVER lend money to friends and family. We give it if we want to—but we don't expect to get it back.

Action 4:   If we are going to have a 15% discount for friends and family, we tell them up front so they understand and there are no issues afterwards—with getting paid or with relationships.

Action 5:   Consider Barter [I'll help you with this, and then you come and help me with what I need].

Gut Feeling

Gut feeling tells us what is right and wrong. NEVER ignore these feelings.

Action 1:   We do not work with anybody that gives us a bad feeling in our gut.

Action 2:   We have our list of people:

- Do not associate with the following…..
- Only associate with the following persons under the following conditions………..
- Associate with the following person AS MUCH AS POSSIBLE…………..

Hiring

Action 1:   All potential employees fill out an application online (on our website if we can host it). We take their social security number and license number and get their approval to do a background check.

Action 2:   We run a background check and a drug test to be sure that the potential employee fits our business model

Action 3:   We have that employee take the pre-employment test to make sure that they have basic Code knowledge.

Action 4:   Employee Handbook so everyone understands the company philosophy and rules of employment. An Organizational Chart so that they understand their role and who their reports are.

Image

The purpose of "image" is of the highest importance; it conveys professionalism; it communicates to everybody the quality of work the customer can expect.

Action 1:   Vehicles must at all times be clean and the inside organized as much as possible.

Action 2:   All employees must comply with the dress code.

Action 3:   Our employees are our sales force; we might be able to get the job the first time but we can't get the second job without our employees that are out in the field.

Insurance

Action 1:   Once a year, we take the time to research, to see if we can re-price our insurance policies; auto, w/c, liability, etc.

Inventions

Nobody cares about our ideas!

Action 1:   We don't invent anything. When we've achieved success, we'll go on our crusades and do our inventions.

Inventory

Action 1:   We will not get a warehouse to store our stockpiled inventory just because we can get it at a discount. We'll create a spreadsheet to determine our needs to see at what point it might become necessary to buy in bulk and store it.

Action 2:   We do critical thinking. Consider buying in advance, have our vendor/supply house store it, and deliver as we need it.

Invoicing Systems

We must have a system.

Action 1:   Consider Fresh Books or other accounting systems. All invoicing must be done immediately.

Action 2:   Have a pricing model and a system in place to track invoices, payments, etc.

Job Costing

The entire business is driven by knowing our cost and profit margin on every job and the running job average. Not only does job costing act as a measure of the accuracy of our estimating abilities, but of our success and failures of project management as well.

Action 1:   Before we can bid on a job we need to have an accurate estimate to determine the cost of the job.

Action 2:   Have a pricing model.

Action 3:   Every job is to be job cost, with weekly summary available.

Labor Units

Have a labor unit manual, learn how to use an estimating system and understand labor units. We must know our labor units before we can bid a job.

Action 1:   If we don't have labor units, we'll do a job, and work it backwards. Make our own worksheet with our own labor units that are appropriate for our business. Of course if this is the first or one of the few jobs of this type that we are doing, we know that going forward we will be able to do the job for less and in less time—adjust our own labor units accordingly.

Action 2:   Only if we are good with spreadsheets and we are doing the same type of work over and again, will we create our own excel spreadsheet and customize our own estimating system

Legal Recourse

Action 1:   I will become an expert on Construction Lien!

Action 2:   I will take every legal means that I can to ensure that I collect on monies owed to me (even if I have no other recourse but to send them a 1099 on December 31st.!)

Lifestyle—Paycheck

Just because we have a business doesn't mean we can afford to live like we do!

Action 1:   Follow our business model, keep our eye on the trends, and change course daily.

Action 2:   Don't forget to respect the guys that work for us or the people in the offices of our vendors or suppliers; build our relationships by honoring the work that they do, don't expect anything in return, but we **will** see the returns.

Marketing

Marketing is the only way to get the word out about our service.

Action 1:   The marketing manager is to ensure that all marketing funds are analyzed as to cost effectiveness.

Action 2:   Business directory ads are to be placed in all newspapers in the areas within 45 minutes of home as measured by GPS.

Action 3:   Billboard Signs are to run for one year to create brand awareness.

Action 4:   Job site signs to be placed on jobs lasting two or more days.

Action 5:   Most advertising requires about 90 days in place to see if it is effective. Efforts should be as direct as possible. Make sure that we are working within the budget that we have created.

Mentor

Find someone who we feel knows more than we do, and "follow" them so that we can learn from them. Use them as a model. Watch who they associate with, and associate with the same people, or the same kind of people.

Negotiation—Dropping Our Price

We will at all times give the customer the best price the first time.

Action 1:   Bid price is to take into consideration the market, the job risk, attitude of the customer, job duration, overtime, travel distance, labor skill and availability, projected cost of material and labor, overhead, and profit. Once a price is given, that is the fixed price.

Action 2:   We will adjust the bid price if additional information is provided that could help reduce the cost to the customer, such as the customer assumes some of the project tasks, like trenching.

Network

Network with our "tribe"

Action 1:   Take advantage of other people (our competition). Stay on a personal level, share information—don't consider our competition as our enemy. We'll be able to share jobs, employees, and information that can make our life easier and our business flow better.

Action 2:   Consider joining industry associations and the Chamber of Commerce. They typically schedule meetings, trade shows and produce many worthwhile publications.

Action 3:   Become active in social organizations to give ourselves an opportunity to be known and demonstrate our professionalism and leadership qualities.

Action 4:   Always be mindful of our time. Don't let associations take more time than we can afford. Never allow external commitments to control our schedule to the detriment of our business, or equally vital, our private life.

"NO"

We cannot bid on every job, we cannot please everyone.

Action 1:   We must learn to say "no". There is a right time to say no to a business opportunity. This can be one of the most difficult things to get, but with practice we'll find it easier to draw the line tactfully and protect our time, and sometimes our money.

Operations Manual—For Each Employee and Process

It is critical to have an Operations Manual so that we can have a consistent way of operating our business—our customer will know what to expect each time, and our employees know what to deliver—according to OUR standard.

Action 1:   Create a manual with every procedure and process in detail. This will help if an employee is out so that there will be no interruption in that service.

Action 2:   Take our time developing this manual. It is a work in progress and needs to be continually updated as we grow and learn.

Organization and Planning is No. 1

We are so busy doing that we are not planning.

Action 1:   Take the time to think out the project and the process and what we need and what time we have in order to complete it.

Action 2:   Make a proper plan and be fully prepared before we start the job.

Other

Action 1:   We do not try to invent anything with the thought of making money, we do it for fun.

Action 2:   We don't waste our time or mental capacity on conspiracy theory; we stay focused on the business model.

Overhead

Many businesses fail because they assumed their business would continue to grow but they had fixed overhead that could be not sustained when business slowed down.

Action 1:   Fixed overhead expenses are only permitted when approved by Finance.

Action 2:   Office rental should be short term, and NO personal guarantees!

Action 3:   Where possible, have shop located at home; when necessary build a home warehouse.

Owners Pay

We may not be able to pay ourselves what we think we should be paid.

Action 1:   Our business model should allow us to get paid what we should earn— but we may have to take less than that and defer "owner benefits" until our business is able to afford to it.

Action 2:   No-one should be working for free, not even our spouse if they are in the business with us.

Payment Terms

Payment policy is to ensure we have the cash flow necessary to fund all projects and pay vendors on time.

Action 1:   All customers are to pay for service at the time of delivery (COD).

Action 2:   Contract work requires a payment draw schedule.

Action 3:   Purchase orders are permitted for property managers, but payment must be made within 30 days of billing.

Action 4:   Any account that doesn't pay their bill on time, or gives a bounced check will no longer receive service.

Action 5:   If our business gets big enough we will consider a system (for example ACH, or ARIBA) which will allow us to sign up (small fee) and transfer money from one account to another without having to accept checks.

Action 6:   I will not lend money to anyone. I might give it but then I will not expect to get it back.

Payroll and Taxes

If we are a one-person business, or a small one, we'll use a company like Intuit to do payroll and taxes.

Action 1:   NO ONE should take money out of the business; pay our employees on time and stay current with payroll taxes.

Permits

Action 1: We will not pull a permit for anybody if we are not doing ALL of the electrical work.

Action 2: Customer to pay for permits.

Personal Finances Program-Savings, Emergency Fund, Retirement

Our personal financial goal is to be debt-free.

Action 1: We work towards paying off all debt and only purchase what we have the cash to purchase.

Action 2: We have a Financial Plan.

Action 3: We read books and attend seminars such as Dave Ramsey to get motivated and learn how to be financially free.

Personal Laws

Action 1: We take a deep breath and wait 5 minutes after any stressful action.

Action 2: We do not respond to a negative text, voice mail, or email for any reason. We consult with someone else before responding if any response is necessary at all. If a response is required, wait 24 hours.

Action 3: No purchases to be made within 24 hours of initial interest and only after consulting with Finance.

Action 4: Personal savings are not to be used for any expenses unless approved by Finance.

Pricing—Emergency Service Call (one man)

The goal of our Emergency Service pricing model is to encourage the customer to "schedule" the call at another time. In addition the pricing model is to include time-and-half for overtime, so that all other calls can get completed as promised.

	1-Man	2-Men
Within 30 minutes of travel First hour	$100 hr	$125 hr
Within 45 minutes of travel First hour	$110 hr	$140 hr
Within 1 hour of travel First hour	$115 hr	$165 hr

Pricing—Scheduled Service Call (one man)

The goal of a service call is to not make money, but to develop a long-term relationship.

	1-Man	2-Men
Within 30 minutes of travel First hour	$75 hr	$100 hr
Within 45 minutes of travel First hour	$90 hr	$115 hr
Within 1 hour of travel First hour	$105 hr	$130 hr

Pricing—Service Call to Recent Installation

When a customer calls us on a job that we just completed, they expect that we'll not charge them with the install we just completed (we all feel this).

Action 1: Make it clear to them that if it's related to our work, then there is no charge for the service, but if it's not related to our work then the cost is as listed above.

Action 2: Verify the phone conversation via text and/or email with the price if it's not our fault.

Action 3: If it's not our fault and we didn't have to go out of our way to stop by, we can discount the service call fee, but this is a judgment call we make at the conclusion of the service.

Action 4: Factors to consider include how much work have we done for the customer in the past? How likely we'll do work form them in the future? Will they be a good referral? How much effort was it on our part? How busy are we? What is their attitude? And our gut feeling…

Pricing—Trenching Manual

For the time being, charge $5 per foot—medium hard soil. We need to do analysis for all future trenching jobs to further refine this price. Naturally the harder the soil, the softer the soil and the length of the trench, will be a factor.

Pricing—Unit Fixed Pricing

Slow Labor—$90, $80, $70, $60, $50, etc.
Normal Labor—$95, $85, $75, $65, $55, etc.
Busy Labor—$100, $90, $80, $70, $60, etc.
Material—20% markup

Plus Trip charge	Slow	Normal	Busy
Travel within 1-15 minutes (one way)	$0	$10	$20
Travel within 16-30 minutes	$10	$20	$30
Travel within 31- 45 minutes	$20	$30	$40
Travel within 46-60 minutes	$30	$40	$50

Products Sold—Water Filters, LV Lighting, Surge Protection

If we are a service contractor and want to get into a concept of selling product, we first take the time to learn what we can do, what we enjoy doing, and which areas we want to focus on. To sell products we have to have a passion to be a salesperson/dealer of products, or hire people to do this for us. Or it becomes a retail venture which takes an enormous amount of energy and capital to run.

Profit

All bids are to include a profit margin approved by Finance.

Action 1: Slow—15%

Action 2: Normal—20%

Action 3: Busy—25%

Action 4: If our price is market price, and we are GOOD, and complete the job early, and our profit is higher, that's OK. As we get better and better at doing the same type of job, our profit will be higher.

Action 5: We do want to try to be consistent with our profit margin in the way we job cost. However, we will find unexpected circumstances (profit more, or profit less) that we can't plan for. It is related to the risk that we take.

Reading Books

If we never read a book on personal development, where could we expect to be years from now? How would we expect to grow?

Action 1: READ. *The Slight Edge*, *The E-Myth*, *Guns, Germs, and Steel* are a good start.

Scheduling

The business model is designed to "under promise" to the customer and to "over deliver".

Action 1: Never "plan" any job to start after 4 pm; this gives us some flexibility during the day.

Action 2: Make it a policy to rarely work past 8 pm; don't accept work that would take us past that time [tired, long day, can make mistakes or get hurt]

Secession Plan

Whenever I think I want to go out of business, I stay in business for 4 years, and then close! [We could probably sell our business for 4 times the profit of a year, and by staying in business for 4 years, make that same money, and still have our business!!]

Action 1: Get someone to operationally run the business so that I can extend my life in the business and still have control of the business but have the life that I want. I can continue to own my business and do what no-one else in the company can do [sales, development and marketing, for example].

Action 2: I will renew my energy, enjoy it more, contribute more, and maybe even make more money.

Service: GFCI, AFCI, LV Lighting, Security, Phone, Cable, Power, Lightning Protection, Sound, Video

Action 1:   Decide what kind of work we want to do and like to do.

Action 2:   Get good at what we do

Action 3:   Don't buy equipment or storage space until we are committed to this line of service.

Slow Periods

During a slow-down in business, to ensure that the business continues to function, it will be required to take "negative" actions [scale down] so that it survives.

Action 1:   Reduce or eliminate benefits.

Action 2:   Reduce salary.

Action 3:   Reduce hours of employment.

Action 4:   Lay off employees.

Stress

Stress is dangerous to our health, and reduces life expectancy; it results in poor performance, lack of desire, poor decision making, and emotional instability.

Action 1:   I'll make a list of all the things that cause me stress

Action 2:   I'll remove recurring stress events ASAP

Action 3:   If the stress is caused by all the jobs and tasks that I have to do, then I need to make sure that they are all on a list, prioritized and then scheduled, IN WRITING. Put everything on a calendar.

Action 4:   I won't stress about the results; just always make sure that I am doing the best that I can do.

Action 5:   I don't associate with anybody that gives my gut a bad feeling.

Action 6:   I'm honest at all times.

Action 7:   We'll follow the business model. We created it to give us a guide—working according to our plan will reduce our stress.

Action 8:   We will have sufficient business and personal savings.

Action 9:   We do not return a call, text, or email to ANYBODY if they cause us stress.

    a. Call our mentor for advice.

    b. We'll respond AFTER 24 hours of consideration.

Surveys

The only way to continue to grow and improve is to listen and learn. Asking for feedback on our performance can improve our business.

Action 1:   We create a customer survey so we can understand what we do well and what we did wrong on each job so that we can learn and do a better job each time.

Action 2:   We have an employee survey so we can better understand their needs and communicate our needs in a clearer way so that we can run our business in a consistent manner.

Taxes and Forms

This is the most important expense and never to be neglected.

Action 1:   We will pay and file all Federal returns on time.

Action 2:   We will pay and file all State returns on time.

Technology

Important to be up to speed with technology

Action 1:   We'll have a website that is outstanding; have a mobile version if possible.

Action 2:   We'll have the right phones to communicate with staff in the field.

Action 3:   Have the right equipment in our office to make life easier—copy machines, scanners, etc.

Action 4: Consider if GPS tracking fits in our business model. If our crew has smart-phones consider getting an app to do it.

Action 5: Make sure that we have rules in place for use of business and personal phones on the job, out of the vehicles, etc. If one of our employees has an accident while using a phone on the job (vehicle, on the ladder, etc.) our company is LIABLE.

Television

There is probably a correlation between really successful people and the amount of television that they watch!

Tools

Having the proper tools and having them 100% in operation is required. If a tool is required to be used three or more times a year, it should be purchased.

Action 1: Less than $100—immediately

Action 2: Over $100—with approval of financial manager

Trip Charge

	Slow	Normal	Busy
Travel within 1-15 minutes (one way)	$0	$10	$20
Travel within 16-30 minutes	$10	$20	$30
Travel within 31- 45 minutes	$20	$30	$40
Travel within 46-60 minutes	$30	$40	$50

Vacations

Vacation is one of the really important benefits. It allows our employees to have time away from the business, refresh and regroup. We will continue to offer a vacation benefits package as long as the business can support it.

Warranty

Work performed by us for a new installation will remain under warranty for a period of one year and work performed by us for service and/or repair will remain under warranty for a period of 90 days.

Action 1: We will call all customers during the month of January to update contact records and ensure that the installation has no failures.

Action 2: Customers that have electrical problems because of faulty wiring by us (not equipment) after warranty period will receive service at no charge.

Action 3: Customers that have electrical problems because of equipment failure supplied by us after warranty period will be charged a service call at standard rates.

Website—Partners Page

Action 1: I will use a professional webmaster to ensure that my website is the best that it can possibly be.

Action 2: I will spend some time visiting other sites and find the features that I like and think are effective, and I will find a way to incorporate those ideas into my site.

Action 3: I will establish a Partner page on my website that is an integral part of my networking efforts

What Have I Done Today To Improve Myself?

Action 1: On a daily basis I will ask myself what I have done today to improve myself and write it down.

Action 2: On a daily basis I will read 10 pages of a business or self-improvement book.

Action 3: On a daily basis I will do at least one thing better than I did yesterday. Something that is easy to do, but also easy not to do (the Slight Edge).

Business Development Worksheet

This worksheet is a summary of all the Action Steps used in the previous Business Model example. It would be used along with that business model to help the person determine which topics they want to focus on for the coming year. After you've created your business model action guidelines, make a worksheet like this to help you analyze where you are and to track your progress.

	My Notes	How important is this? #1, #2, #3	Currently: where do I see myself? (rank 1-10, 10=best)	A Year from Now: where do I want to be? (rank 1-10, 10=best)
Accounting System				
Actions				
Aging Report				
Bad Checks				
Banking/Banker				
Barter				
Bids				
Bills				
Bonus				
Business Expenses versus Personal				
Busy Times				
Change Orders				
Codes & Standards				
Communications				
Continued Education				
Continuous Improvement				
Contract Conditions				
Contract Work—Owner				
Contract Work—General Contractor				
Credit Card Usage				
Crusades				
Customer Type/Selection				

	My Notes	How Important Is This? #1, #2, #3	Currently: Where Do I See Myself? (rank 1-10, 10=best)	A Year From Now: Where Do I Want To Be? (rank 1-10, 10=best)
Daily Log				
Discounts				
Draw				
Dress Code				
Employee Relationships				
Employment				
Equipment				
Estimating Systems				
Family				
Friends				
Finance				
Gut Feeling				
Image				
Insurance				
Inventions				
Inventory				
Invoicing Systems				
Job Costing				
Labor Units				
Lifestyle—Paycheck				
Marketing				
Mentor				
Negotiation				
Operations Manual				
Organization and Planning				
Other				
Overhead				
Owners Pay				
Payment Terms				
Payroll and Taxes				

	My Notes	How Important Is This? #1, #2, #3	Currently: Where Do I See Myself? (rank 1-10, 10=best)	A Year From Now: Where Do I Want To Be? (rank 1-10, 10=best)
Permits				
Personal Finance Program				
Personal Laws				
Pricing—Emergency Service Call				
Pricing—Scheduled Service Call				
Pricing—Service Call/Recent Install				
Pricing—Trenching Manual				
Pricing—Unit Fixed Pricing				
Products Sold				
Profit				
Quotes—Slow				
Quotes—Normal Work Load				
Quotes—Busy				
Reading Books				
Service				
Scheduling				
Slow Periods				
Stress				
Stressed Out				
Surveys				
Taxes				
Technology				
Television				
Tools				
Trip Charge				
Vacations				
Warranty				
Website—Partners Page				
What did I do TODAY to improve myself?				

Daily Log Example

Did you ever wonder where the day went and you feel like you have nothing to show for it? A Daily Log can assist you and/or your employees review your day, identify what's keeping you from meeting your goals, and help you be more productive. If you find this list too long for your needs, choose the items that are most important. When you rate, use a scale of 1-10, 10 being the highest.

Performance/Activity

Rate your job management skills _____ If not 10, why not and what can you do differently?_____

Rate your electrical installation performance _____

If not 10, why not and what can you do differently? _____

Started administrative work _____ Finished administrative work _____

Arrived at first job _____ Left final job _____

Hours billed for the day _____ Non-productive time _____ Why?_____

What tool would have made the day more productive?_____

What positive thoughts did you have today?_____

What negative thoughts did you have today?_____

Did you complete the check list with the customer? ☐ No ☐ Yes

Did you email the customer a thank you with survey? ☐ No ☐ Yes

What new LAW did you create today?_____

What LAW did you break today?_____

What lesson did you learn today and why?_____

What materials would have made the job easier?_____

What inventory was purchased and stored?_____

Phone Call Data

calls/leads received today? _____

of these calls/leads done today? _____

# of these calls/leads scheduled service? _____

How many of these did you give a price only? _____

How many of these were a total waste of time? _____

Lead Source Data

Billboard _____

DexKnows _____

Local paper_____

Other (describe)_____

Repeat _____

Van/Truck _____

Website _____

Marketing

What did you do today to help the business in securing more work?_____

What did you learn today that can help the business get more work?_____

What should you have done today to help the business get more work?_____

How many pages did you read today?_____

Organizational Chart Example

At first glance this might not seem useful to you if you are a small business, or even a one-man shop. However, what we've tried to illustrate here is that all these functions are important for a business to run smoothly and be successful. Make a copy of this page, and on each line below the business function, write the name of the person responsible. If your own name appears on many, or even all of the positions listed below (assuming they are appropriate for your type of business) you'll have a better understanding of your role. Your goal is to do the best that you possibly can to get the job done.

Organizational Structure

A business (even a one man shop) has to have an organizational structure, with each position identified as to its responsibilities and how it interacts with each department.

Owner

Responsible for making as much money as possible with the least amount of effort.

Chief Executive Officer

Ensures that each VP is doing their job and that company policy is developed, managed and applied.

VP Operations

At all times ensures that all jobs are done efficiently and effectively in a manner that is profitable, yet meets customer's total satisfaction.

VP Finance

Ensures proper cash flow. Is responsible for taxes, insurances, bonds, licensing, weekly income report (data from PM submitted to the COO), monthly net worth report (data from AR and AP submitted to COO) and payroll.

VP Marketing

Ensures company is promoted on the internet, newspapers, and possibly direct mail. Continues to explore ways to market the company with the least amount of cost. Works with Finance and Production to measure effectiveness of marketing plan. Is responsible for company image.

Production Mgr.

Ensures all electricians in the field are skilled for the job and professional at all times (including uniforms). Develops a service checklist for the field staff and ensures it is followed, with daily report forwarded to COO. Responsible to supply VP of Finance weekly income reports as well as job costing for each job daily. Ensures all customers are billed at the end of the job and pay immediately, unless approved otherwise by VP Finance. Ensures all vehicles have sufficient inventory, but not more than needed.

Accounts Receivable Mgr.

Ensures that all customers have paid according to the terms agreed to in advance, and reports any past due accounts immediately to the VP of Finance.

Sales Mgr.

Responsibility is to "sell the job", ensuring that the job is profitable (min 15% profit). Must consult with VP of Marketing (who consults with Ops & Finance VPs) for any jobs that have a value of over $10,000 to ensure that STS can manage the job (production) and that the company has the cash flow (finance). In addition, the Sales Manager is responsible for the company's reputation.

Field Electricians

Accounts Payable Mgr.

Pays all bills in a timely manner and notifies VP of Finance anytime an invoice is questionable.

Advertising Mgr.

Reports to VP Marketing, working in conjunction or assisting Sales Manager as necessary.

Cust. Service Mgr.

Requests testimonials from all customers and forwards to VP Marketing; calls to follow up on customers, handles complaints to the customer's complete satisfaction.

Reports

Reports to AP, AR, VP Finance, as necessary.

Facilities Mgr.

Ensures that all tools required by the production manager are available and in good working order. In addition, is responsible for vehicle maintenance and repairs.

Customer Survey Example

If you're looking for one tool that can transform your business, this is it! Embrace what your customers think and say about your company [the good together with the bad]—it will help you build a better business. The example below has many questions, and for the most part your customers will not want to take the time to answer too many questions. Create your own survey—choose the questions from below that you feel work best for you, or use our example to come up with others that better evaluate the customer experience for your type of business.

Did we meet or exceed your expectations?　☐ No　☐ Yes

How could we improve? _____

_____

Did we respond timely to your phone calls or emails?　☐ No　☐ Yes

How could we improve?_____

_____

Did we complete your job in a timely manner?　☐ No　☐ Yes

How could we improve?_____

_____

Were you satisfied with our communication?　☐ No　☐ Yes

How could we improve? _____

_____

Did the installation meet with your total satisfaction?　☐ No　☐ Yes

How could we improve? _____

_____

Were we courteous and professional at all times?　☐ No　☐ Yes

How could we improve? _____

_____

If the need arises, will you use our service again?　☐ No　☐ Yes

Why? _____

_____

Would you recommend us to your friends?　☐ No　☐ Yes

Why? _____

_____

Would you be willing to receive inquiries on the service received?_____

Employee Survey Example

Don't under-rate the value and opinions of your employees. They are the ones in the trenches on a daily basis and might see a lot more than you do. Taking the time to survey your employees has more benefits than you might first think. A survey helps your employees feel that the work they are doing contributes to the overall success of the business; it helps you get completely different perspectives; it takes some of the burden off yourself to solve all the problems alone; helps you get more commitment to the solutions. Remember, if you don't act on their suggestions let them know why not, or your survey loses its value. The following is an example of a weekly survey:

What equipment were you missing this week that could have made your job easier?

_____

_____

What problems did you have this week with customers? _____

_____

What was the problem? _____

_____

How can we solve it?_____

_____

What lost time happened on the job and why? _____

_____

Is there anything we can be doing so that this does not happen again? _____

_____

What did we get right this week? _____

_____

How can we use that experience to improve other things in the company?_____

_____

Was there anything that disappointed you this week? _____

_____

Do you need training in any area that will help you do your job better?_____

_____

Proposal for Electrical Work
Example 1

[Your Company Logo]   [Your Company Address]

[Your Company Tagline]

PROPOSAL FOR ELECTRICAL SYSTEMS

_____ is honored to provide a proposal of pricing in accordance with the electrical specifications and terms and conditions identified on page 2 of 3, and electrical calculations contained in page 3 of 3.

This proposal becomes a binding contractual agreement when signed by both parties.

[Proposal Date]		
Contractor/Owner Contact Information		
[Company, Website]		
[Contact, email, phone]		
[Address, city, state, zip]		
Job Information		
[Job Name]		
[Job Address, City, State, Zip]		
Power Systems		**Cost**
Electrical Power with Decora Switches and Receptacles		
Living Space Area (square foot)		
Credit for standard grade switches and receptacles.		
Low Voltage and Limited Energy	**Outlets**	**Cost**
Telephone Outlet (Cat 5)		
TV Outlet—One Coaxial Cable		
Data/Internet Outlet (Cat 6)		
Closed Circuit Television (CCTV)		
Security System with Two Control Panels		
Sound System (ceiling speakers with volume control)		
Other Options		**Cost**
Generator 17 kW Air Cooled w/200A Transfer Switch		
Surge Protection (power, cable, and phone)		
Temporary Wiring		

Builder/Owner Name: _____ Date: _____/_____/_____

Contractor Name: _____ Date: _____/_____/_____

p 1 of 3

Electrical Specifications

1. Codes—Material and equipment will be provided and installed in accordance with the National Electrical Code®, the Florida Building Code, and standard electrical practices.

2. Devices (switches and receptacles)—Devices shall be of the Decora type in the color white unless otherwise instructed in writing. Receptacles will be installed vertical with the ground prong down unless otherwise instructed in writing.

3. Lighting—Bid price includes builder grade recessed cans and builder grade fluorescent fixtures according to plans.

4. Safe Work Practices—All electrical work will be performed in accordance with OSHA and NFPA 70E® safe work practices. *No electrical work will be performed within or on equipment that is energized.*

5. Warrantee—Bid price includes one-year warranty for electrical equipment, lighting fixtures supplied by Premier Power, Inc., excluding bulbs, and wiring.

6. Service—Bid price includes one 200A 120/240V single-phase service meter/main disconnect, but no service conductors from the meter/main to the utility transformer.

7. Panel(s)—Bid price includes one 200A 120/240V panel supplied with SER aluminum 250 kcmil cable.

Note: Where the service and/or electrical panel location is not identified on the plans and/or specifications, bid price is based on 50 feet of SER cable between the service meter/main disconnect and electrical panel.

8. *Conductor Material.* Copper conductors for circuits rated under 100A and aluminum for 100A or larger.

7. Height—Switches, lights, and receptacles will be installed as follows unless notified otherwise in writing:

- **Switches**—Approximately forty-four inches from the bottom of the box to finished floor/grade.
- **Lights (wall inside)**—Approximately seven feet from the bottom of the box for 10' ceilings to the floor and six feet to the bottom of the box for 8' ceilings to the floor.
- **Lights (wall outside)**—Approximately six to seven feet from the bottom of the box to the outside grade.
- **Receptacles**—Indoors—Approximately twelve inches from the bottom of the box to the finished interior floor. Outdoors—Approximately twenty-four inches from to the bottom of the box to the outside grade.

Terms and Conditions

1. Concrete—Bid price does not include concrete or paint.

2. Changes—Alteration to the scope of this agreement or wiring modifications due to errors in design will only be executed upon receipt of written priced and signed work order.

3. Notice to Owner—[_____] will serve a notice to the owner in accordance with §713.06, Florida Statutes.

4. Payment and Terms—Payment is due within 14 days of invoice date in accordance with the following draw schedule:

- Slab Electrical Inspection Approval—5% of total contract price
- Rough Electrical Inspection Approval—45% of total contract price
- Meter and Service Disconnect Electrical Inspection Approval—15% of total contract price
- Final Electrical Inspection Approval—35% of total contract price

5. Performance—Bid price is based on all work performed between 7 am—5 pm Monday—Friday, excluding legal holidays. Work requested after 5 pm on weekdays or anytime during a weekend will only be performed upon receipt of a written priced and signed work order.

[_____] will not perform any electrical work in accordance with this contract during the period an invoice has not been paid in accordance with this agreement.

6. Permit—The cost of the electrical permit is not included in the bid price.

7. Schedule—[_____] requires no less than five business days' notification for each of the job phases; in addition [_____] requires the following time for electrical installation after the plumbing and mechanical contractors have completed their work:

- Slab—2 days
- Rough—8 days
- Meter and Service Disconnect—2 days
- Trim—4 days

8. Termination of Agreement—Either party can terminate this agreement prior to the installation of any wiring shown on plans.

[Your Company Logo]   [Your Company Address]

[Your Company Tagline]

Electrical Service Calculation

General Lighting and Receptacle Circuits	Qty		VA Load	
General Lighting and Receptacles @ 3 VA per square foot				
Lighting Outlets				
Switch Outlets				
Receptacle Outlets				
Kitchen Circuits				
Laundry Circuit				
Appliances	**Qty**	**Run**	**VA Load**	
Air-Conditioning 3-Ton, 12 AWG, 240V Circuit				
Air-Conditioning 5-Ton, 10 AWG, 240V Circuit				
Cooktop 30A, 240V Circuit				
Dishwasher, 15A, 120 Circuit				
Disposal, 15A, 120 Circuit				
Dryer, 30A Circuit				
Electric Heat 7.5 kW, 40A, 240V Circuit				
Electric Heat 9.6 kW, 50A, 240V Circuit				
Microwave, 20A, 120V Circuit				
Oven Single, 30A, 240V Circuit				
Oven Double 40A, 240V Circuit				
Range, 50A, 240V Circuit				
Water Heater 30A, 240V Circuit				
Well, 20A, 240V Circuit				
Service Calculations				
Total Connected Load without A/C and Heat				
First 10 KW at 100% demand				
Remainder at 40% demand				
Net Computed Demand Load				**VA**
System Voltage				**V**
Minimum Service in Amperes				**A**

p 3 of 3

Proposal for Electrical Work
Example 2

Date of Submission: _____

Proposal submitted by: _____

_____

_____

Proposal submitted to: _____

_____

_____

Job information: _____

_____

_____

Scope of work: _____

_____

_____

Plans and Specifications:_____

_____

_____

[Proposal is based on the submitted plans, with revisions as indicated.]

Your Company Name proposes to furnish the aforementioned material and/or labor in accordance with the above conditions for the sum of _____Dollars ($). Proposed price shall remain in effect for a period of _____months from the date of acceptance. Any work required under this proposal after this date is not covered within the scope of this proposal.

Payment Schedule: Payments to be made as listed above. Payments not received by invoice due date shall be considered past due. Past due accounts will be charged an interest charge at the rate of 1.5% per month until the balance is paid in full. No release of lien shall be signed unless all payments are paid in full.

Signed By: _____ Title: _____ Date: _____

This is your authorization to complete the work as outlined above according to conditions on the front and reverse sides of this proposal.

Acceptance Signed By: _____ Title: _____

Print Name: _____ Date: _____

When both parties sign this proposal, this instrument constitutes a legal and binding contract between the parties. This proposal may be withdrawn if not accepted within fifteen (15) days from date of submission.

p. 1 of 3

NON-COMPETE CLAUSE: Owner and all authorized representatives of Owner are not to contract or employ any contractor employees for a period of one (1) year from the completion of any electrical work performed by this Contractor with said Owner/Agent within an area of fifty (50) miles radius from this job site.

PERFORMANCE: Your Company Name agrees that where a written construction schedule is provided with the signing of this proposal and fails to comply with said schedule, **Your Company Name** shall pay all overtime costs necessary to complete construction in a timely manner.

If a written construction schedule is not provided with the signing of this proposal, **Your Company Name** shall not pay for any overtime to complete project and any overtime required shall be considered an extra and authorization shall be required according to CHANGES AND EXTRAS referred to below. Reasonable time shall be given to **Your Company Name** to complete each phase of the electrical job.

MATERIALS AND EQUIPMENT: All material and equipment shall be as warranted by the manufacturer and will be installed in a manner consistent with standard practices at this time. It is agreed that title to all material required (for the purpose of this proposal) to remain the property of Your Company Name until paid in full. It is understood that Your Company Name shall have the authorization to enter upon owner/contractor property for the purpose of repossessing material and equipment whether or not installed without liability to owner/contractor for trespass or any other reason.

EXCLUSIONS: This proposal does not include concrete, forming, painting, patching, trenching, core drilling, venting and sealing of roof penetrations. All waste created by electrical contractor will be removed to a specific area on the construction site.

CHANGE ORDERS: Any deviation, alteration or changes from this proposal will be executed only on receipt of written work order. Said charges shall in no way affect or make void the proposal. Charges for changes or modification to this proposal will be based on a labor rate of forty-five ($45.00) dollars per man-hour. This labor rate includes labor, labor benefits, supervision, overhead, warranty, and other cost. Material shall be charged at contractor's list price.

Your Company Name must receive written authorization by any of the individuals listed below prior to commencement of the work. NO WORK SHALL COMMENCE UNTIL THIS ELECTRICAL CONTRACTOR RECEIVES WRITTEN AUTHORIZATION.

Individual authorized to sign written change orders shall be:

Name: _____ Title: _____

Name: _____ Title: _____

NATIONAL AND LOCAL CODES: Electrical installation shall meet the *National Electrical Code* and local building codes. Errors in design by the architect and/or engineer are not the responsibility of **Your Company Name**. Any additional outlets, wiring, fixtures, equipment, etc. not indicated on plans and specifications that are required by other (i.e., Inspectors) shall not be part of this proposal.

FIXTURES AND EQUIPMENT SUPPLIED BY OTHERS: *Price includes* the installation of fixtures furnished by others, if fixtures are on job at time of electrical trim out. Fluorescent fixtures supplied by others shall be assembled, pre-whipped, and pre-lamped with in-line fuses.

Electrical Contractor shall not be responsible for fixtures and equipment supplied by others and losses due to theft, damage, vandalism, etc. are not the responsibility of **[Your Company Name]**. Fixtures and equipment must be stored by others. *Price does not* cover:

(1) The warranty of fixtures and equipment supplied by others.
(2) The assembly of fixtures and/or equipment supplied by others.
(3) Fixtures weighing more than fifty (50) pounds.
(4) Equipment supplied by others (except fixtures according to conditions above) shall be installed by others.

p. 2 of 3

WARRANTY: *Warranties shall apply* exclusively to the electrical installation of the material, fixtures, equipment, and other items supplied by the electrical contractor. *Warranty does not apply to:*

(1) Material, fixtures, equipment and other items supplied by others.
(2) Extensions or additions to the original installation if made by others.

Warranty shall commence from the final electrical inspection date for a maximum period of one (1) year. Warranty or service will not be performed if any payments according to this proposal become past due including change orders.

ELECTRICAL CONTRACTOR SHALL NOT BE LIABLE: For failure to perform if prevented by strikes, or other labor disputes, accidents, acts of God, governmental or municipal regulation or interference, shortages of labor or materials, delays in transportation, non-availability of the same from manufacturer or supplier, or other causes beyond electrical contractor's control. In no event shall the electrical contractor be liable for special or consequential damages whatsoever or however caused.

OWNER/CONTRACTOR DEFAULTS: Owner/contractor will be in default if:

(1) Any payment called for under this proposal and all authorized change orders become past due.
(2) Any written agreement made by the owner/contractor is not promptly performed.
(3) Any conditions warranted by the owner/contractor prove to be untrue.
(4) Failure of owner/contractor to comply with any of the conditions of this proposal.

Electrical contractor's remedies in the event of owner/contractor defaults, in event of owner/contractor default, electrical contractor may do any or all of the following:

(1) Suspend the work and remove its material/equipment from the premises.

(2) Remove any Electrical Contractor-supplied material/equipment, whether or not it has been installed and whether or not is has been placed in operation. In this regard, owner/contractor agrees that electrical contractor may enter upon owner/contractor property for the purpose of repossessing such equipment without liability to owner/contractor for trespass or any other reason.

(3) Retain all monies paid hereunder, regardless of the stage of completion of the work and bring any appropriate action in court to enforce its rights. The owner/contractor agrees to pay all costs and expenses, attorney's fees, court costs, collection fees (including fees incurred in connection with appeals) incurred by electrical contractor in enforcing its rights under this proposal.

Electrical contractor carries Workers' Compensation and Professional Liability Insurance covering its work on this job. Owner/contractor agrees to notify his/her insurance company of the commencement of work. Risk of loss due to fire, windstorm, vandalism, or other casualty shall be upon the owner/contractor.

p. 3 of 3